# Minority Students in STEM Careers in the U.S. – the Role of AP Calculus

By Dr. Kendall Edsal Coleman

B.S, 2000, Prairie View A&M University, Texas

M.B.A, 2012, Governors State University, Illinois

M.A.U.M., 2015, Trinity International University, Illinois

Ed.S., 2019 National-Louis University, Illinois

Ed.D., 2019 National-Louis University, Illinois

## DEDICATION

This work is dedicated to my mother, Elma J. Coleman, a retired Chicago Public School (CPS) teacher, my dad Louis Coleman who worked for the Chicago Transit Authority (CTA), my siblings, and for future generations of family members, students, the community, and public service workers.

ACKNOWLEDGEMENTS

I am thankful for the insightful expertise and guidance provided to me by my dissertation chair Dr. Agnieszka A. Hanni. I also want to thank National Louis University for the opportunity to study at this institution of higher education.

ISBN -13:    978-0-578-70805-8

**Dr. Kendall E. Coleman**

P.O. Box 19381

7715 S. Cottage Grove Ave. Suite 1

Chicago, IL 60619

Book Cover Artwork by Dr. Kendall E. Coleman

Interior Design by Dr. Kendall E. Coleman

Dr. Kendall E. Coleman's graduation from National-Louis University for a Doctorate in Higher Educational Leadership (Ed.D) and Educational Specialist (Ed.S) degrees

Minority Students in STEM Careers in the U.S. - the Role of AP Calculus

## Biographical Sketch

From K-12th grade, Kendall Coleman attended school within the Chicago Public School System (CPS). In high school, Kendall took courses in electronics, computer-aided design, and programming at Chicago Vocational High School (CVS). Kendall knew that he wanted to major in engineering by the time he graduated from high school based upon the classes he took. At CVS, the highest level of mathematics offered at that time was college algebra. He could not take calculus as it was not an option. What Kendall did not know was that the majority of the college-level engineering courses would require him to take calculus as a prerequisite. As a result, he began his college engineering program academically-behind with a deficit in mathematics even though he graduated in the top 10% of his class. He would have to spend additional time catching up to other students in order to meet the rigorous academic standards of the program. After completing his B.S. degree in electrical engineering, Kendall worked for IBM and Seagate Technology as a senior engineer, and completed two Masters degrees with one of them being in business administration (MBA). Kendall holds certifications in project management (PMP), OSHA 511, ITILv3, and chaplaincy. Currently, Kendall teaches Computer Science for the Chicago Public School System.

ABSTRACT

"The number of native-born S&E [science and engineering] graduates entering the workforce is likely to decline unless the nation intervenes to improve success in educating S&E students from all demographic groups, especially those that have been underrepresented in S&E careers" (National Science Board [NSB], 2003, p. 13). More than a decade ago, the National Science Board (NSB) sounded an alarm regarding the projected decline in native-born science and engineering graduates with the aim of driving strategic fundamental changes. There is limited evidence that the NSB's prognostication is actively being addressed. Approximately 81% percent of all full-time graduate students in U.S. electrical engineering programs are international students with 79% of them majoring in computer science (Redden, 2017). The U.S. will need 1 million STEM professionals over the next 10 years to fill a growing domestic economic demand (Xue & Larson, 2015). "Mathematics preparation may be particularly critical since at many colleges, readiness for college-level calculus is a prerequisite to admission for quantitative majors" (Oakes, 1990, p. 14). As of April 2019, approximately 48 undergraduate bachelor degrees at Saint Louis University required students to take Survey of Calculus or Calculus 1 as a prerequisite for meeting graduating requirements in STEM majors. According to the U.S. Department of Education (DOE), students who took high school calculus and expressed interest in STEM careers had the lowest attrition rate in college (U.S. Department of Education [DOE], 2014). Research from the Federal Reserve Bank of Cleveland indicates that students that took advanced mathematics in high school received a greater economic return throughout their life-time (James, 2013; Thompson, 2013). This study used correlations and regression tests to determine that the educational attainment of the parent's was statistical significant in predicting

high school calculus completion. The research data set from the DOE contained approximately

18,922 high school students from across the nation. If the parent's highest level of education was

a high school diploma then only 8.54% of the children took and passed high school calculus in

comparison to 44.08% of the children of doctorate graduates that took and passed calculus.

Keyword:   Math, Calculus, Education, STEM, Careers

TABLE OF CONTENTS

CHAPTER

CHAPTER 1

INTRODUCTION

**Institutional Study**

St. Louis University (SLU) in Missouri a private, Catholic, Jesuit higher education institution, was founded in 1818 as St. Louis College (St. Louis College, 1904; Garraghan, 1983). In 1832, SLU was granted a charter by the legislature of Missouri to confer degrees in all of the learned occupations (St. Louis College, 1904). The mission of SLU "is the pursuit of truth for the greater glory of God and for the service of humanity" (Wisdom & Levitt, 2015, p. 412). The university seeks to develop future leaders, to understand God's creation, to share values and knowledge to transform society to reflect the Gospels of Christ. SLU encourages academic studies in the arts, humanities, medical sciences, social sciences, law, and aviation. Higher education through institutions such as SLU serves the public good for the benefit of society (Hansmann, 2012).

Problem Statement

In 2017, SLU's medical school was placed on probation for its inability to recruit diverse candidates along with issues associated with curriculum, oversight, and outcome data centralization by the Liaison Committee on Medical Education (LCME) (Jost, 2017; Liaison Committee on Medical Education [LCME], 2017). According to the U.S. Department of Education (DOE, 2014), African-Americans and Hispanics had the lowest completion rate of AP calculus. Underrepresented minorities may lack the necessary mathematical preparation to succeed in the STEM programs at Saint Louis University.

The SLU Medical Scholars program provides an opportunity for highly motivated students to receive early acceptance into the SLU School of Medicine. The program allows first-year students to gain out-of-classroom experience in medicine. One interesting caveat of the program is that all SLU Medical scholars must take Calculus I, and AP credit to satisfy the

requirement (SLU, 2018).

Several B.S. degrees at Saint Louis University require that the student take calculus for

subjects such as accounting, finance, geology, information technology management, electrical

engineering, biochemistry, biology, computer science, chemistry, and computer science. If a

student has taken high school AP calculus, it is easier for him/her to advance through the

coursework. Incoming freshmen into the institution must take a mathematics placement

examination. At SLU, the majority of incoming freshmen had an ACT score of 27 compared to

the national composite average of 20.8.

Table 1

*SLU ACT Scores of Admitted Students*

|  | Applied | Admit | Enroll |
|---|---|---|---|
| ACT Average | 27.0 | 27.5 | 27.6 |
| 75th % | 30 | 30 | 30 |
| 25% | 23 | 24 | 24 |

*Note.* Data retrieved from the SLU 2015-2016 Fact Book.

## Purpose of Study

The purpose of this study is to identify relationships that exist between the variables of

parental income, parental education, student completion of high school calculus, student

gender, and student race to increase access to calculus to underrepresented minorities.

According to the U.S. Department of Education, those who take calculus in high school and

express interest in STEM have the lowest dropout rate of those enrolled in college (DOE,

2014; DOE, 2012).

## Assumptions

A detectable mathematical achievement gap between various racial groups exist within the U.S. in the third or fourth grade (NAEP, 2017). Negative subconscious attitudes toward mathematics develop at an early age (Cohen & Rubinsten, 2017). In some cases, invisible environmental, psychological, systematic forces may exist that adversely affect a child's attitudes toward mathematics (Cohen & Rubinsten, 2017). Psychological biases that stipulate that everyone is not good at math reinforce psychological barriers that counteract a student's willingness to engage in repetitive constructive productive struggle (Dickerson, 2013).

## Research Questions

The research questions explored in this study were:

1. Does a parent's higher level of education increase the likelihood that his/her child will take and pass calculus in high school?

2. Does a father's education or mother's education have a greater influence on a child's decision to take calculus in high school?

The research questions aim to illuminate the factors and correlations that may increase the likelihood of a student taking AP calculus in high school and graduating with a STEM degree from a university such as Saint Louis University.

## Hypotheses

- A parent's higher level of education increases the likelihood that his/her child will take calculus in high school. **[HYP: A]**

- The mother's education is a greater predictor of a child taking calculus in high school than the father. **[HYP: B]**

CHAPTER 2

LITERATURE REVIEW

The literature review elucidates existing research that sought to answer questions

surrounding high school calculus, attrition, attitudes, and economic factors. The questions that

this research study aims at addressing seeks to understand the factors that influence the taking

of calculus. Very little if any existing research has focused on the mathematical achievement

gap that exists within the City of Chicago, the third largest school district in the United States.

**Participation of Women in STEM careers around the world**

According to the World Economic Forum (WEF, 2018), nations with higher gender

equality have an uneven representation of women in science, technology, engineering, and

mathematics (STEM) careers. Scientists refer to this phenomenon as the gender-equality paradox

because countries with the greatest participation of women in the workforce have the lowest

participation of women in STEM fields (World Economic Forum, 2018).  In a study conducted

by the WEF analyzing data from 475,000 adolescents from 67 countries, it was determined that

males had the highest overall achievements in science while females had the highest overall

achievements in reading.  Reportedly, it is the overall interest in STEM and higher reading

ability of females that contributes to this paradox.  According to the UNESCO Institute for

Statistics, women are less likely to enroll in STEM fields than they are in health, welfare, and

education (World Bank, 2019).

When women earn STEM degrees and enter the workforce, strong cultures of masculinity

have been found to deter their long-term persistence in those careers (Cheryan, Ziegler,

Montoya, & Jiang, 2017). Women earn approximately 37% of all undergraduate STEM degrees

in the U.S., but some STEM fields have more female representation than others (See Figure 1 in

Appendix A and Figure 2 in Appendix B). Specifically, women earn more degrees in the branch

of the biological sciences of STEM than the other areas (Cheryan, Ziegler, Montoya, & Jiang,

2017). Women earn only 30% of undergraduate chemical engineering degrees and 11% of

electrical engineering degrees (Cheryan, Ziegler, Montoya, & Jiang, 2017). (See Figure 3 in

Appendix C). Some of the factors that contribute to women not preserving in STEM careers

may affect the perseverance of underrepresented minorities achieving success in STEM.

### Foreign Students Enrolled in Science & Engineering in the U.S.

Students from China earned the largest number of U.S. S&E doctorates awarded to

foreign students during the 1989–2009 period (NSB, 2012). In the 2012-2013 academic year,

more than 800,000 international students were enrolled in U.S. colleges and universities (Zhu &

Cox, 2015). Researchers utilized ANOVA Statistical Analysis and Perry's Theory of student

cognitive and ethical development in their methodology to understand the epistemological

development of Chinese students enrolled in the U.S. (Zhu & Cox, 2015). They determined that

engineering students develop differently from students enrolled in liberal arts programs in that

liberal arts program students are trained to explore different perspectives while the training of

engineering students is much more rigid. The majority of Chinese students enrolled in the

science and engineering doctoral programs originated from the 'project 211' universities. The

term 'project 211' originated from an initiative by the government of China in 1994 to establish

one-hundred key higher education institutions by the 21$^{st}$ century and underpin them with

billions of dollars (Huang, 2015). The initiative resulted in China boosting 136 of its schools

into the top global 1,250 *US News* rankings, and making China second only to the U.S. in articles

and citations in STEM and number one in material science (Li, 2018). In a few years, the U.S.

may no longer be number one.

To rate the epistemological development of Chinese students in the U.S., researchers constructed a survey that analyzed dualism and commitment (Zhu, & Cox, 2015). The survey was administered to 1,000 Chinese engineering students attending several Midwest universities in the U.S. Doctoral students appeared to exhibit highest levels of critical thinking on a survey that rated students on a scale from 1 to 5. Freshmen undergraduate students had a rating of 2.61, senior students had a rating of 3.31, master degree students had a rating of 3.82, second-year master degree students had a rating of 4.13, and doctoral students had a rating of 4.30 (Zhu, & Cox, 2015). The research elucidated the differences in the students' ability to engage in productive struggle and higher order thinking based upon degree level. According to the principles of the depth of knowledge (DOK) opined by Norman Webb, the greatest range of complexity, cognitive rigor, extending thinking, and planning occurs at the level of DOK 4 (Karuguti, Phillips, & Barr, 2017), which supports Zhu & Cox's (2015) research. Norman Webb was a research science at the Wisconsin Center for Education at the University of Wisconsin-Madison (Webb, 1997). Advanced mathematics is associated with strong critical thinking skills.

The enrollment of international students in the U.S. declined by 2.7% in 2018 (Redden, 2019). Changes in the U.S. stance on immigration and geopolitical transformations lead some international students to reconsider studying in the United States (Saul, 2018).  Visa applications came under greater scrutiny following the 2016 presidential election (Saul, 2018).

### International PISA Mathematics

As of 2015, the U.S. ranked 40th among 70 other nations on the International Programme for International Student Assessment (PISA) Mathematics test for 15-year-olds (PISA, 2015). The highest possible score is 600 points (Serino, 2017). Leading the group was Singapore with an average score of 564 out of 600 points followed by Hong Kong with a score of 564 (China),

Macau scored 544 (China), Chinese Taipei scored 542, Japan 532, BSJG (China) scored 531, the

Republic of Korea scored 524, Switzerland scored 521, and the U.S. scored 470. The top seven

nations were all located in Asia. Other nations that achieved a higher score than the US include

Spain, Italy, Portugal, France, the Russian Federation, Vietnam, Austria, and the United

Kingdom. By international standards, the US educational system has fallen behind and has

reached a dire state (Bolick, 2017) (See Figure 4 in Appendix D).

**Participation of International Students in STEM Careers**

The Australian Council of Learned Academies (ACOLA) commissioned a research report

to compare the country of Australia with the other nations of the world to understand STEM

enrollment in the academic domains, access of STEM to various labor markets, and the relevance

of STEM to the economic growth of the Australian nation (ACOLA, 2013). The ACOLA

gathered data from the country of Australia, regional reports, and the Organisation for Economic

Co-operation and Development (OECD) to understand STEM on the global level.  In terms of

methodology, various university professors were tasked with researching different countries such

as China, Taiwan, Japan, Singapore, Korea, the United States, Canada, Western Europe, Finland,

France, the United Kingdom, New Zealand, and Russia to develop reports regarding STEM

education in their nations. The authors of the reports were from different universities around the

world such as the University of Melbourne, Osaka University, University of Minnesota, Indiana

University, Clemson University, Kings College London, and the University of Auckland.

In 2012, OECD reported that within the United States of America, 64% of all college

graduates earn non-STEM degrees, and only 18.42% graduate with a degree in engineering,

manufacturing, and construction (ACOLA, 2013) (See Figure 5 in Appendix E). As a

comparison, in the country of Sweden, 48.26% of the students graduate with a non-STEM degree, and 34.51% graduate with a degree in engineering, manufacturing, and construction (ACOLA, 2013). OECD strives to improve the socioeconomic condition of people around the world. It was founded December 14, 1960, and consist of 36 different member countries around the world such as Australia, Belgium, Canada, Denmark, Japan, Norway, Mexico, Korea, Turkey, New Zealand, the United Kingdom, and the United States. The group is founded by member countries.

## STEM Careers Representation in the U.S.

The Pew Research Center is a think tank that informs the public about issues and attitudes shaping the nation and world through public opinion polls, demographic studies, and data-driven social science (Pew, 2018). The Pew Research Center is a subsidiary of the Pew Charitable Trust, which was founded in 1948. In terms of methodology, the Pew Research Center surveys people through landline and cellular phones. Nearly 25% of interviews are conducted by landlines and 75% are conducted by cellphone. When the Pew Research Center contacts candidates they first ask if they are 18 years old. The sampling error for 1,500 surveys is +/ 2.9% with a 95% statistical confidence interval (Pew, 2019).

About 52% of all STEM jobs, 9 million, are in healthcare. According to the Pew Research Center, STEM employment has grown 79% from 1990 -2016 with computer jobs increasing by 338% (Pew, 2018). African-Americans represent 11% of the workforce of the US, but only holds 9% of the STEM degrees, and Hispanics represent 16% of the workforce and hold only 7% of the STEM jobs. Surprisingly, 17% of all college-educated STEM US workers are Asian whereas only 10% of the US population works in STEM (Pew, 2018). According to the US Census, Asian American's are only 5.6% of the population (U.S. Census, 2010). The US Asian Population grew by 72% from 2000 -2015 (Lopez, Ruiz, & Patten, 2017). In the US, 51%

of all Asians 25 years old and older have a bachelor degree, and 72% of Indians Asians living in the US hold a bachelor degree (Lopez, Ruiz, & Patten, 2017).

According to the Pew Research Center, African-American STEM professionals believe that limited educational opportunities, discriminatory recruitment and promotion, and a lack of exposure at an early age contribute to inequalities (Funk, & Parker, 2018). Approximately, 57% of African-Americans believe that their workplace does not pay enough attention to increasing racial and ethnic diversity in comparison to 15% of Caucasians. African-American and Hispanics made up 27% of the U.S. workforce in 2016, but only 16% worked in STEM (Funk, & Parker, 2018) (See Figure 6 in Appendix F, and Figure 7 in Appendix G).

### U.S. Department of Education

College completion in the STEM fields remains a problem within the US (DOE, 2014). The National Center for Education Statistics (NCES) collects, analyze, and report data related to the condition of education within the United States of America to identify trends and provide consistent information to policymakers. Data from the US Department of Education indicates that students who expressed an interest in STEM and took AP Calculus in high school had the lowest attrition rate in college and were less likely to switch into a non-STEM field (DOE, 2014) (See Figure 8 in Appendix H). The students that had the second lowest attrition rate were those that took pre-calculus in high school. Students that took advanced mathematics in high school were more likely to complete a STEM degree (Tyson, Lee, Borman, & Hanson, 2007; Wang, 2013).

**Human Capital Theory**

Human Capital has been defined as the knowledge and resources that one embodies (Becker, & Tomes, 1985; Ployhart, Nyberg, Reilly, & Maltarich, 2014). The educational attainment and socioeconomic status of a parent influences the educational investments into their children (Bainbridge, Meyers, Tanaka, & Waldfogel, 2005; Hao, & Yeung, 2015). Within education, "the learning of complicated mathematics and other materials are more efficient when the building blocks of elementary concepts are mastered" (Becker, & Tomes, 1985, pg. 326). According to the tenets of Human Capital Theory, as conceptualized by Gary S. Becker (Becker, & Tomes, 1985), education improves income equality, increases the efficiency of workers, reduces bottlenecks in economic growth, and diminishes the scarcity of skilled labor (Teixeira, 2016). The educational achievement of a parent influences the socioeconomic advancement of child (Sommer, Chase-Lansdale, Brooks-Gunn, Gardner, Rauner, & Freel, 2012).

A father's education attainment strongly influences the child's academic success (Adams, 2014). Additionally, some children have a special advantage over other children because their families have greater ability, emphasize childhood learning, and because of the family culture (Becker, & Tomes, 1985). The earnings of children depend in large part on the earnings of their parents. Children of higher income earning households more educational support (Bainbridge, Meyers, Tanaka, & Waldfogel, 2005). Socio-economic factors will limit the volume of Human capital dollars that African-American and Hispanic individuals may devote toward their children since underrepresented minorities tend to earn less than their white male or female counterpart (Becker, & Tomes, 1985). (See Figure 9 in Appendix I)

Students that earned a two year associates degree earned more money than high school graduates (Torpey, 2018). Inequality in labor supply curves and earnings could be reduced through human capital investments in educational subsidies to public schools, need-based scholarships, and government-funded head-start programs for poor children. The wealth of parents contributes to inequality among children (Becker, & Tomes, 1985). Market force discrimination creates income inequalities and influences intergenerational poverty (Bloome, 2014). The decline in two parent households has contributed to income inequality (Bloome, 2017). Structural macroeconomic changes has altered the dynamics of underrepresented minorities and women in the workforce over the past decades (Toossi, 2002). On many college campuses, the number of women outnumbers the number of men (Marcus, 2017). African-American women earn 60% of the degrees awarded to African-American (Mcdaniel, Diprete, Buchmann, & Shwed, 2011).

## Income Inequality

The U.S. ranks very high among industrialized nations for income inequality (Odgers, & Adler, 2018). In a study conducted by Akee, Jones, and Porter (2019) that analyzed income inequality and mobility in the U.S. from 2000-2014 using U.S. Census data and I.R.S. tax records, Caucasians and Asians had the highest income in the nation. Researchers utilized income indices, the Shorrocks Index, Gini coefficient calculator, and income ratios to create graphs of the data. The Shorrocks index compares short and long-run income inequalities in society. More income leads to higher levels of mobility (Akee, Jones, & Porter, 2019). For the year 2000 and 2014, African-Americans had the highest level of immobility in the nation compared with all other racial groups. Approximately 60% of African-Americans that started in the lowest-income quintile in 2000 remained at the same low economic quintile in 2014. African-Americans and Hispanics were more likely than any other racial groups in the nation to slide backward into lower income quintiles (Akee, Jones, & Porter, 2019).

African-Americans, Hispanics, and Native Americans were the lowest income earning group, they had the highest probability of experience diminishing mobility, and were less likely to file income taxes. For the purpose of this study, the data included 94% to 96% of the tax-filing population. The U.S. 2010 Census count included 166 million observations. In the year 2000, 128 million individuals filed I.R.S. tax form 1040, and in 2014, 137 million people filed I.R.S. tax form 1040 (Akee, Jones, & Porter, 2019).

Income inequalities may contribute to differences in the quality of life and life-span of various groups (Odgers, & Adler, 2018). African-Americans have a life expectancy that is four years shorter than their white counterparts with infant mortality rates being 140% higher (Akee, Jones, & Porter, 2019). African-American to Caucasian homeownership differed by approximately 23%. Even when African-Americans earn a college education, income disparities continue to exist. Income inequality across the entire U.S. grown at twice the Gini Index from 1967-2012 (Gastwirth, 2014). The gap between the rich and poor has increased by 40% - 50% over the past forty years (Odgers, & Adler, 2018). Income mobility decreased for all racial and ethnic groups between the time frame of 2000 and 2014 due to the 2008-2009 global financial crisis also known as the Great Recession (Akee, Jones, & Porter, 2019). Additionally, African-American, Hispanics, and American Indians tend to have less earnings mobility than other racial groups. A rigid income structure has existed in the U.S. for decades. The study produced by Akee, Jones, & Porter (2019) sheds light on the college attrition rate of Hispanics and African-American since numerous researching finding by the U.S. Department of Education and National Science Foundation showed links between socio-economic status and college degree attainment (DOE, 2014). Asians had the highest percentage of people as a share of their population as the top 10% of income earners in the U.S. for the year 2000 and 2014 (Akee, Jones, & Porter, 2019).

Educational attainment increases overall household income (Torpey, 2018). The SES of a child is strongly influenced by the SES of the parent (Odgers, Adler, & 2018). In the year 2000 for the top 1% income earners in the nation, Caucasians made up 92.10%, African-Americans 0.97%, Hispanics 1.88%, and Asians 4.67%. In the year 2014, for the top 1% Caucasians made 87.83%, African-Americans 1.39%, and Asians 7.16% (Akee, Jones, & Porter, 2019). While the data shows a small negligible increase in the percentage of African-Americans that made up the top 1%, the study did not provide a source of their income. It would prudent to if these individuals were business owners, medical doctors, entertainers, or athletes. (See Figure 10 in Appendix J).

## Self-Determination Theory

Human capital theory and self-determination theory provides a framework for understanding educational attainment, income inequality, intergenerational poverty, motivation, and psychological biases. Self-determination theory deals with the cognitive motivation and beliefs of humans as they interact with their environment. In a study conducted by research scientists that included n=754 Norway students in higher education biology throughout the country, scientists sought to predict the probability of dropping out of school based upon self-determination theory (SDT). Autonomous motivation and self-perceptions of competency strongly correlated with a student's ability to persevere. Effective teacher to student feedback and optimally challenging assignments that increased with rigor ameliorated a student's perceived level of competency (Jeno, Danielsen, & Raaheim, 2018). As the student builds self-confidence in their ability to perform tasks successfully, they tend to work harder in performing more challenging tasks.

In a self-determination study conducted by Paixão, & Gamboa, (2017) which sought to understand the motivation of N=396 high school students in Portugal (175 teenage boys and 221 teenage girls) with the mean age of 17.02 in the 11$^{th}$ and 12$^{th}$ grade using self-determination theory researchers were able to offer a conceptual framework for predicting the motivation in a students' career decision making deliberation. Career exploration plays a significant role for students nearing the end of their high school years as they determine whether to pursue a college education, enter the workforce, or engage in a hybrid of both (Paixão & Gamboa, 2017). A complex higher order process takes places as students' reflect on their self as it relates to their external environment, career commitment, and adaptability.

Supportive engaging environments provide antecedents. Self-determination originates from intrinsic and extrinsic motivation which explains the ability of an individual to adjust to their environment. Intrinsic motivation grows from a person's internal interest, reward system, competency, and pleasure (Paixão & Gamboa, 2017). Extrinsic motivation must balance intention with reward, punishment, anxiety, and guilt. The methodology that Paixão and Gamboa utilized incorporated standard deviation, charts, mean, minimum, maximum, and range. Paixão and Gamboa (2017) citing a research study conducted by Jung (2013) that analyzed the self-determination of N= 349 high school students recommended for the educational community and students' to develop strategies to motivate their children.

Expectancy-Value theory is a subset or composite of self-determination theory. According to Expectancy-Value Theory, mathematical achievement could be understood through the lenses of expectations and values that students hold about mathematics (Priess-groben & Hyde, 2017).  Mathematical motivation tends to decline for many youths during the high school years. Students that exhibited an ability to sustain an interest in mathematics tended to take more college-level classes that involved math rigor than students whose interest declined. According to Implicit theory, a person carries a certain set of psychological biases that enable them to believe or disbelieve that they can improve in any academic subject such as mathematics (Priessgroben & Hyde, 2017). (See Figure 11 in Appendix K).

**Federal Reserve Bank**

In April 2019, the Federal Reserve Bank released a report that explored employment opportunities for Sub-Baccalaureate jobs across the United States (Federal Reserve Bank, 2019). The researchers at the Federal Reserve Bank concluded that students without a college education earned a median income of $37,690 adjusted for small regional differences that accounted for 21% of the total measured employment within 121 different metropolitan areas. The largest opportunity areas for growth included healthcare and skilled trades, which may experience above-average growth. The level of opportunity varied by the region with Toledo, OH receiving the highest at 34.0% compared with Washington, DC, receiving the lowest at 14.6%. Some jobs required a bachelor degree such as registered nurses, accountants, and operational managers, while other occupations such as tractor-trailer truck drivers, plumbers, and construction laborers.

The Federal Reserve Bank used information from the May 2017 Occupational Employment Statistics, the U.S. Labor Bureau, and the Burning Glass Technologies research database that contained info on 75 million job ads to produce its data (Federal Reserve Bank, 2019). From the data, one may deduce that individuals with a college degree will earn more money and compete for jobs that pay a higher overall salary. Additionally, in the city of Chicago and nationwide, nursing has become the number one job opportunity and STEM relation position according to the Federal Reserve Bank (2019) (See Figure 12 in Appendix L).

Table 2

Top Ten Opportunity Occupations in 2017 for Chicago-Naperville-Elgin, IL-IN-WI

| # | Position | Annual Median Wage | Opportunity Employment |
|---|----------|--------------------|------------------------|
| 1 | Registered Nurses | $74,300 | 57, 600 |
| 2 | Heavy and Tractor-Trailer Drivers | $49,000 | 52,600 |
| 3 | Maintenance and Repair Workers | $41,700 | 44,400 |
| 4 | Construction Laborers | $58,400 | 24,700 |
| 5 | Police and Sheriff's Patrol Officers | $83,000 | 24,200 |
| 6 | Bookkeeping, accounting, and clerks | $41,500 | 22,900 |
| 7 | Sales representatives, wholesale and manufacturing | $60,600 | 19,300 |
| 8 | General and operations manager | $122,900 | 19,200 |
| 9 | Automotive service technicians and mechanics | $43,400 | 19,100 |
| 10 | Carpenters | $71,300 | 18,900 |

## Pre-school & College Degree Attainment

According to the CLS, which collected data from an intervention of group of 989 preschools and a comparison group 559 pre-school children in Chicago, IL, children that attended pre-school were more likely to graduate from high school, obtain a higher level of college readiness, and attend college (Topitzes, Godes, Mersky, Ceglarek, & Reynolds, 2009). The racial makeup of the CLS participants was 94% African-American and 6% Hispanic. According to a longitudinal study of preschool and adult IQ, the more mental development that child receives in infancy, the stronger their IQ level will be later on in life (DiLalla & Thompson, 1990).

## Barriers to Academic Success

Underrepresented minorities that graduate from college will pay more for the same degree than their white counterparts because underrepresented minorities will need to take out more student loans to pay for their education (Kim, Chatterjee, Young, & Moon, 2017). This would be similar to two people walking into a car dealership to purchase an identical car, and one person will need to pay double what the other person pays because they were a minority. Yet the factors that contribute to the differential that exists between Caucasians and African-Americans in student loans may have more to do with family household income, single family head house versus two parent house, the educational attainment of the mother, and environmental conditions.

Some African-American & Hispanic parents contribute less to their child's college education than Caucasians (Kim, Chatterjee, Young, & Moon, 2017). If every parent could send their child to college free or could fully pay for their child's education, then some of the current economic disparities would diminish. If African-Americans graduate with more student loan debt than Caucasians, then African-American college graduates will be less likely to own a house and car. The U.S. student loan debt has reached trillions of dollars. Minorities tend to leave college with greater student loan debt than their white counterparts (Kim, Chatterjee, Young, & Moon, 2017). If someone goes to college and drops out without completing their degree, that raises the risk of default. The more student debt that an individual has, the less likely they will be to own a home (Kim, Chatterjee, Young, & Moon, 2017). Underrepresented minorities face unique challenges that represent barriers to achieving the American dream and attaining a college education.

## Compulsory Math Coursework

Economists have theorized that additional years of schooling raises income (Goodman, 2012). For every additional year of mathematics that an African-American male takes, he raises his earnings by 5-9% which closes a fifth of the earnings gap that exists between white and African-American students (Goodman, 2012). Prior research has not extensively explored the links between mathematical achievement and labor force outcomes. Changes in the high school graduation requirements increased the quantity of African-Americans taking calculus in high school. Each U.S. state has a different requirement for the number of years of

mathematics that a student must take to earn a high school diploma (Goodman, 2012).

For a variety of reasons, a mathematical achievement gap exists between various racial

groups in the United States. African-American male students take less rigorous math courses

than Caucasian students, have lower math skills than Caucasian students, or some variation of

the two factors (Goodman, 2012). Part of the reason that underrepresented minorities take less

rigorous math courses may originate from access, and the other part choice (Goodman, 2012).

Even when given the option to take more rigorous courses, some students chose not to. When

the African-American student took more advanced math classes in high school, they earned more

money in the labor force (Goodman, 2012) (See Figure 13 in Appendix M).

## AP Calculus and Future Income

According to the Federal Reserve Bank of Cleveland students that took advanced

mathematics in high school will see greater economic returns throughout their life-time than

students that did not (James, 2013; Thompson, 2013). A correlation exist between advanced

high school mathematics and labor market outcomes (James, 2013; Thompson, 2013). A greater

percentage of Asian and Caucasian students take high school calculus than African-American

and Hispanics (DOE, 2014). By taking one year of calculus in high school, the African-

American male student can dramatically alter the amount of income earned in their life (Battey,

2013). Additionally, underrepresented minorities receive fewer referrals from high school

counselors to take AP calculus possible do to a lack of mathematical achievement (Battey, 2013).

Battey (2013) analyzed national data sets from 1982, 1992, and 2004, and explored racial

privileges through the dimensions of institutional, labor, and identity.

Employers struggle to fill about 48% of the jobs referred to as middle-skill which require

in some cases college-level mathematics classes (Kochan, Finegold, & Osterman, 2012). Over

the past decades, the U.S. business community has strived at revamping K-12 science and

mathematics education to reduce the intercity drop-out rates. Congress lacks the political will to

realistically drive constructive changes on a large national scale. Targeted incentives from the

federal government directed toward local and state programs may close the skills gap (Kochan,

Finegold, & Osterman, 2012).

In a research study conducted by Byun, Irvin, & Bell (2015), they demonstrated using the

U.S. Department of Education longitudinal data that by taking advanced math courses in high

school, students experienced greater mathematical achievement and college enrollment. Nearly

every college major requires the completion of a math course. As students take more rigorous

high school classes, they will become more prepared for the rigors of college (Byun, Irvin, &

Bell, 2015). Advanced mathematics coursework may also increase occupational opportunities for

an individual from socio-disadvantaged backgrounds. Perhaps college enrollment increased

because admissions counselors viewed the taking of calculus in high school as a positive

contributor to college success. Students that had parents that earned a Master's or Doctorate in

college were more likely to take calculus in high school than students that only earned a

Bachelor degree (Barshay, 2015). Less than 10% of students took calculus if the parent only

obtained a high school diploma (See Figure 14 in Appendix N).

Differences in access affects the participation rate of Hispanics and African-Americans in

high school. Underrepresented minorities have unequal access to rigorous high school courses

(Perna, May, Yee, Ransom, Rodriguez, & Fester, 2015). In terms of methodology, researchers

drew upon information from the International Baccalaureate (IBDP) data that contained information from 400,000 students from 1995 – 2009 and common core data from the U.S. Department of Education's National Center for Education Statistics data. In some instances, if an underrepresented minority wanted to take an advanced mathematics course they could not. Personal self-esteem and motivation may propel a student to preserve through difficult course content.

Confident students are more likely to excel in engineering than less confident students (Litzler & Young, 2012). Several questions may arise regarding why certain students appear more confident than others in certain content. Oftentimes, knowledge increases the confidence of facts. The more knowledge that a student has regarding key concepts, skills, and the course learning outcomes the more confident that they will become. A student without a firm grip of the facts may display lower confidence in the content (Litzler & Young, 2012). Student empowerment may increase confidence (Chambers, Walpole, & Outlaw, 2016; Kirk, Lewis, Brown, Karibo, & Park, 2016).

Two different K-12 models exist for educating the underrepresented disadvantaged minorities within the United States (Wax, 2017). The first model aims to reduce the number of underperforming schools that segregate by socioeconomic status and racial background and expand opportunities for more students to attend middle class and affluent institutions. The second model seeks to create clusters of K-12 high intensity 'no-excuse' charter schools. When underperforming students are placed in high performing environments they tend to do better, but the results have been mixed in terms of graduating from college. Even though the students did better in K-12, it did not automatically lead to degree completion. The higher performing 'no excuse' schools with students from low socioeconomic backgrounds tended to outperform similar students in public education by only 3% on standardized exams. No excuse schools are high expectation schools with strict code of conducts in predominately low income areas. Middle-class children underperformed in selective charter schools, only lower income students tended to perform better (Wax, 2017).

## Project-based STEM of Faculty

Post-secondary instruction into STEM could be supported through project-based training of faculty members (Asghar, Ellington, Rice, Johnson, & Prime, 2012). Students need constant psychological engagement that involves exploration, inquiry, problem solving, and critical thinking to remain interested in STEM subjects. Rich cross-disciplinary experiences strengthen knowledge of science and mathematics (Asghar, et al., 2012). Several US states have launched reforms in teacher education to train them in cross-disciplinary instructional strategies. The teacher-centered training in Maryland sought to understand the evolution of teacher perceptions, challenges associated with implementing STEM project-based learning, and possible directions for future professional development (Asghar, et al., 2012).

## Suskie Quality Framework

In the book, *Five dimensions of quality: A common sense guide to accreditation,* Suskie, (2014) provides insight into changes that occurred within higher education beginning with the 1965 Title IV Higher Education Act (HEA) (p. 16). The act sought to establish financial aid programs with the stipulation that students must attend colleges and universities accredited by entities sanctioned by the U.S. Department of Education (DOE). The accreditors functioned as gatekeepers. Every few years, the DOE would raise the requirements for accreditors who would, in turn, raise the requirements for academic institutions. In the 1980s, accreditors began to demand that institutions fulfill their stated mission or reason for existence. The 2008 Higher Education Opportunity Act (HEOA) sought to address insufficiencies associated with the rigor of prior accreditation standards to be more outcome driven, measurable, and transparent (Suskie, 2014). Accreditors exist in large part to serve the public good, ensure a certain standard of quality exists at every institution, and to protect students as well as taxpayers that indirectly fund the financial aid programs (Suskie, 2014).

The five different cultural dimensions of quality have been categorized as relevance, community, focus, evidence, and overall betterment (Sukie, 2014). The culture of relevance embodies integrity, stewardship, and fiscal management (Sukie, 2014). Academic institutions are continually shaped by a culture of scholarship and relevance (Stanbury, 2010). Within an active culture of evidence, a university would document faculty members' degrees, their professional development growth, and field experiences (Sukie, 2014). An interaction exists between the culture of community, evidence, and relevance. For within the culture of the community, an organization will exhibit respect, fairness, trust, and incorporate students and faculty in their decisions. The leadership of an organization plays a large role in the culture that exists at a school (Hofmeyer, Sheingold, Klopper, & Warland, 2015).

## Culture of Community

Stakeholders play a vital role in any large-scale organization. Saint Louis University has a many different stakeholders banking on the success of the university. The board of trustees of Saint Louis University contains over 40 different leaders representing the fields of finance, business, theology, and industry. The faculty senate would be considered a major stakeholder in the success of the institution. A stakeholder has been defined as a consentient of an organization (Missonier, S. & Loufrani-Fedida, 2014). The stakeholder role in an organization will evolve as the organization evolves (Missonier, S. & Loufrani-Fedida, 2014). In SLU's infancy, the main stakeholders of the programs, products, and services offered by SLU actively participated in the Jesuit tradition as lay members, pupils, and priests (St. Louis College, 1904).

The culture of community that exists at SLU emanates from the shared values of the Catholic Jesuit faith, academic scholarship, the institutional mission, and shared governance structure. A shared governance structure describes the roles of key stakeholders such as faculty members, the board of directors, and the student senates in the governance of the university (Roesler, 2016; Taylor, 2013). At SLU, the board of trustees governs the entire university and appoints the university president. The president oversees the office of diversity, university provost, and dean of medicine (SLU, 2019). At SLU, the Dean of Medicine reports directly to the university president whereas the other deans and vice-presidents report to the university provost.

The term community has been defined as a group of people with diverse characteristics that share social ties and a common perspective (MacQueen, McLellan, Metzger, Kegeles, Strauss, Scotti, Blanchard, & Trotter, 2001). In the culture of a community, mutual respect, honest communication, fair treatment, and trust governs the environment (Suskie, 2014). Information tends to motivate action within a community with a strong culture (Suskie, 2014). Within a culture of the community, a culture of documentation exists that provides clear rules of the game (Suskie, 2014). At SLU, the Catholic Jesuit culture of self-discipline, the pursuit of truth, and community service drive strategic plans.

The five strategic planning initiatives of Saint Louis University consist of the institution exemplifying transformative educational research excellence, establishing market leadership in health promotion and achieving the highest quality medical care, being a catalyst for significant change in the region world, to innovate and pioneer new ideas, and foster a culture of effectiveness that aligns to the university's mission and Jesuit culture (SLU, 2015). SLU's strategic plan contains 22 goals (SLU, 2015). The two goals that underpin the strategic initiative of healthcare are to expand access to clinical services and to take a holistic approach to healthcare research (Petrin, 2017; SLU, 2017). The entire strategic plan may be summarized in five words namely research, healthcare, catalyst, innovation, and Jesuit.

## Culture of Evidence

The core tenants of a culture of evidence will manifest themselves within a higher education institution through its adherence to integrity, transparency, accurate documentation, evidence of student learning, assessments, a curriculum that aligns to the accreditation standards of a governing body, the percentage of students receiving a job in their field of study, the student debt to career field ratio, and evidence of trained faculty members in their chosen field of instruction (Sukie, 2014). Students of SLU will gain knowledge in the curriculum through in-class instruction, hypothesis-based experiments, field experiences, and internships, and co-ops. To successfully maintain and operate the medical school at SLU, the institution must adhere to a set of standards created by the Liaison Committee on Medical Education (LCME). In 2017, the Liaison of Medical Committee placed SLU on probationary status for not maintain the accreditation standards of the LCME (Jost, 2017).

**Latino Doctor Shortage**

A study conducted by Sanchez, Nevarez, Schink, and Hayes-Bautista (2015) analyzed 30 years of data to understand the rate of Latino physicians per 100,000 people. In terms of methodology, the researchers gathered information from the U.S. Census public microdata samples from the years of 1980-2010 to understand the total number of Spanish-language speaking Hispanic and non-Hispanic Caucasian physicians. While the quantity of non-

Hispanic Caucasian physicians has increased over the past 30 years, the quantity of Spanish-language speaking Hispanics has decreased over the same period. Latino physicians had a higher probability of fluently speaking Spanish than non-Hispanic Caucasian physicians. The researchers concluded that a critical Latino doctor shortage has grown worse over the past 30 years (Sanchez, Nevarez, Schink, & Hayes-Bautista, 2015). According to the U.S. Census, 40 million people in the U.S. spoke Spanish at home (U.S. Census, 2017).

### High School Calculus and Attrition in Florida

Tyson (2011), measured the degree attainment of high school students in the state of Florida that who advanced placement classes and found that high school calculus was the greatest predictor of earning a STEM college education (Tyson, 2011). Tyson used a multinomial logistic regression statistical analysis to determine high and low achievement in high school college level physics and calculus (Tyson, 2011). Tyson's first hypothesis sought to understand the switch out rate of college students that took high school AP calculus and physics. His second hypothesis sought to understand the grades of students who took high school physics and calculus, and their corresponding switch out rate in college (Tyson, 2011). The switch out rate deals with students that initially declare a STEM major, but later decide to switch to another. "Tyson (2011) modeled the effects of high school course grades on engineering students' degree attainment in Florida universities during the 2002–2003 school year and found that high school AP Calculus grades were the most effective factor on Physics and Calculus II course performance in college, and students, who took AP Physics B and/or C, showed better performance in Physics and Calculus III in college. Tyson (2011) concluded that high school GPA, calculus, and physics course scores were effective measures to predict the prerequisite course performance in engineering" (Yoon, & Stroble, 2017, p. 2).

## African-Americans' Socioeconomic Status

Numerous studies have shown links between socioeconomic status (SES) and academic performance (Diemer, & Ali, 2009; Reardon, Valentino, Kalogrides, Shores, & Greenberg, 2013). Underrepresented minorities, first-generation students, and low socioeconomic students tend to do far worse academically in STEM majors than others (Doerschuk, Bahrim, Daniel, Kruger, Mann, & Martin, 2016). Socioeconomic status is influenced by the incomes of the parents (Stack, & Meredith, 2017).

In a study conducted by Stack and Meredith (2017), the researchers studied British single families in the United Kingdom (U.K.) and determined that families headed by single parents had a greater risk of financial hardship. A lack of income led to greater stress, feelings of helplessness and hopelessness, decreased social interactions, increased sleepless nights, and depression (Stack, & Meredith, 2017). Participants would do whatever they could to ensure that their children had food even if that meant not paying utility bills. The researchers collected data through two interviews that lasted 30 to 90 minutes in length. Fifteen people participated in the study (n=15). The age of the participants ranged from 18 to 55 years old. The participants worked full-time and part-time jobs. The participants' singleness contributed to their hardship (Stack, & Meredith, 2017).

According to the Bureau of Labor Statistics (BLS) (2019), the unemployment rate of African-Americans was 6.7%, compared with whites which are 3.3%. The unemployment rate of African-American 16-19 year olds was 22.4% compared with whites at 10.9% (BLS). The BLS did not provide a reason for the unemployment disparity that existed between African-American teenagers and other races, and the effects of their unemployment.

In a research study analyzing the correlation between summer jobs and violence (Mervis, 2014), it was determined that African-American teenagers in Chicago who had summer jobs were 43% less likely to commit violent crimes than teenagers who did not have jobs. Even after the summer job ended, they were less likely to commit crimes than those students who did not have a job. In the research study, 730 teenagers were selected randomly for jobs out of a pool of 1,694 applicants. Approximately 95% of the participants in the study were African-American (Mervis, 2014), The teenagers in the study worked 25 hours per week in positions such as a community gardener or camp counselor for eight weeks. Each participant was partnered with a mentor who taught them soft skills in conflict resolution and self-control. Since links exist between socioeconomic status and college graduation (Diemer, & Ali, 2009; Reardon, Valentino, Kalogrides, Shores, & Greenberg, 2013).

According to the Brookings Institute (Winship, Reeves, & Guyot, 2018), African-Americans are more likely to be born into poverty. Intergenerational poverty in the African-American community is largely influenced by the economic outcomes of the African-American male (Scott, Reeves, & Guyot. 2018; Winship, Reeves, & Guyot, 2018) (See Figure 15 in Appendix O). African-American males who are born poor are more likely to remain in poverty more so than African-American women (Reeves, & Rodrigue, 2017).

Chapter Three

METHODOLOGY

Chapter 3 describes the approach taken to describe the data, collection methods, sample

size, hypotheses, and results. This research sought to describe the quantitative relationships that

exist between college attrition and high school calculus in the context of likelihood of future

participation in STEM careers, especially as they relate to participation of minority students.

Correlations, simple regressions and ANOVAs or nonparametric equivalents of ANOVA were

used to analyze data from the U.S. Department of Education's 2009 Longitudinal Study.

**Sample Population**

The DOE longitudinal data set (Table 3) from 2009 includes information of 18,922

students. Approximately 59.95% of the respondents came from households that earned an

income of $115,000 or less per year, 15.26% earned more than $115,000 per year, and

approximately 11% did not indicate family income. The U.S. Department of Education

information is a representative sample of the 15 million students enrolled in $9^{th} - 12^{th}$ grade in

the U.S.

**Governmental Data Sources**

The pragmatist researches problems and identifies solutions within a real-world context

(Creswell, 2013). Quantitative research aims to build an analytical foundation through verifiable,

quantifiable, and elucidated data from data sources such as the U.S. Department of Education

(DOE). The DOE 2009 longitudinal data set takes information from high school students across

the entire nation in both private and public schools.

Beginning in 1968, the U.S. Department of Education's Civil Rights Data Collection

(CRDC) office started collecting information regarding student enrollment, sex, race, ethnicity,

and disability. The online database provides a mechanism to retrieve information by school and perform data analysis. The database automatically produces graphs of information representing such factors as racial breakdown for all public and private schools and participation in calculus, algebra, gifted and talented programs, etc. The current available DOE Civil Rights database contains school district datasets from the years 2000 -2015.

Table 3.

Sources of Quantitative Information

| # | Source | Study | Data Type | Population | Participants |
|---|--------|-------|-----------|-----------|--------------|
| 1 | US Dept. of Education National Center for Educational Statistics https://nces.ed.gov/onlinecodebook | High school longitudinal study of 2009 | Raw data file | 18,922 | high school students |

Note. Description of the sources of quantitative information

**Statistical Tests**

The Levene's Test, the Pearson's Chi-squared Test, the Pearson's Product Moment Test, the ANOVA, and the F-test will be used to evaluate the study. The Levene's test was performed to examine the equality of variances across the considered groups (Soave & Sun, 2017). For any result were the probability falls within the statistical significance ($p<0.05$), the variances for the groups are not equal for normally distributed data in which case a nonparametric equivalent of a t-test may be more appropriate (Wang, Rodriguez de Gil, Chen, Kromrey, Kim, Pham, Nguyen, & Romano, 2017). When the p-value of that test is $\leq 0.05$ the null hypothesis is rejected, when the p value is $> 0.05$, then one fails to reject the null hypothesis.

In the case of the U.S. Department of Education data, the test was used to determine whether high school calculus is offered onsite based upon the family income, race, the father's education, the mother's education, and gender. The data set included a sample of 24,905 students from both public and private schools which represents the 15.1 million high school students throughout the U.S.

## Q-Q Plot

The quantile-quantile plot (Q-Q Plot) provides a graphical representation of data sets with common population distributions (Estudillo-Martínez, Castillo-Gutiérrez, & Lozano-Aguilera, 2013). When plotted points are more or less rectilinear, then the hypothesis of normality could not be rejected. The sample sizes do not need to be identical and distributional aspects can be tested simultaneously. The plot will estimate quantiles of students that earned calculus credit in high school against other variables such as a mother's or father's educational attainment. Q-Q Plots may appear with a right-skew, left skew, under-dispersed, and over dispersed.

## Residuals vs. Fitted

If the model has constant variance, then the Residuals vs. Fitted plot should indicate a random scattering of data points below and above the line at horizontal 0. If the values are not randomly scattered, then this indicates a non-constant variance. The Residuals vs. Fitted plots is a scatter plot measuring data between residuals and predicted values, and it makes it easier to determine curvature and spread across the observations.

## RStudio Software

To perform statistical tests and generate plots from the U.S. Department of Education's 2009 longitudinal data, the RStudio Software package was used. RStudio is an open-source version of R-programming language for statistical computations. Data miners and statisticians use R-programming for polls, surveys, data analysis, regression models, and geo-spatial coordinates, among many other reasons.

## Analyses

- A parent's higher level of education increases the likelihood that his/her child will take calculus in high school. **[HYP: A]**

- The parental education hypothesis underwent a statistical correlation investigation by analyzing the variables of parental education and participation in onsite calculus.

- The mother's education is a greater predictor of a child taking calculus in high school than the father. **[HYP: B]**

  - A simple regression evaluated the mother's education hypothesis by analyzing the variables of mother's education and participation in onsite calculus.

## Study Variables

Out of 9196 number of variables from the original dataset, the researcher selected six variables for this study. Table 4 below provides a snapshot of the variables used. Parent's highest level of education was designated as X2PAREDU in the original data set.

Table 4.
Variables Used for Data Analysis of Dept. of Education 2009 Longitudinal Study

| | |
|---|---|
| X2PAREDU | Parents'/guardians' highest level of education |
| X2MOMEDU | Mother's/female guardian's highest level of education |
| X2DADEDU | Father's/male guardian's highest level of education |
| X1SEX | Students sex male 1 or female 2 |
| X1RACE | Students race White, America Indian, Asian, Black, Hispanic, two or more |
| X3T1CREDCALC | At least one credit earned in Calculus |

The parental education variable of X2PAREDU represents the highest educational level achieved by either parent #1 or parent #2. There were eight educational categories measured by the DOE such as less than a high school (1,094 parents), high school diploma or GED (6,400 parents), certificate /diploma from occupational training or trade school (1,011 parents), associate's degree (3,342 parents), bachelor's degree (5,154 parents), master's degree (2,615 parents), doctorate (1,303 parents), and missing (2,594 parents). For the mother's variable of X2MOMEDU there were nine categories which represent the highest level of education achieved by the mother living in the household regardless as to whether the mother was a biological, an

adoptive father or a step-mother. The nine categories entailed: no bio/adoptive/step-mother in

household (1,530 households), less than high school (1,576 mothers), high school diploma or

GED (7,160 mothers), certificate /diploma from occupational training or trade school (829

mothers), associate's degree (3,108 mothers), bachelor's degree (4,476 mothers), master's degree

(1,674), doctorate (566 mothers), and non-response/missing (2,584). For the father's variable of

X2DADEDU, there were nine categories which represent the highest level of education achieved

by the father living in the household regardless as to whether the father was a biological, an

adoptive father or a step-father. The nine categories entail: no bio/adoptive/step-father in

household (5,193 fathers), less than high school, high school diploma or GED (1,461 fathers),

certificate /diploma from occupational training or trade school (557 fathers), associate's degree

(1,941 fathers), bachelor's degree (3,333 fathers), master's degree (1,411 fathers), and doctorate

(872 fathers), and unit non-response/missing (2,584)

The data associated with the variable of X1SEX originated from a DOE student-, parent-,

and school-provided questionnaire in which the student was either identified as a male or female.

Approximately 11,973 or 50.94% of the students were male and 11,524 students or 49.03% of

the students were female, and 6 or 0.03% of the students did not select a category. For the

variable of X1RACE, there were eight categories of students identified as: American

Indian/Alaska Native (165 students), Asian non-Hispanic (1,952 students), Black/African-

American non-Hispanic (2,450 students), Hispanic no race specified (422 students), Hispanic

race specified (3,375 students), More than one race non-Hispanic (1,941 students), Native

Hawaiian/Pacific Islander non-Hispanic (110 students), and White non-Hispanic (12,082), and missing (1,006 students). Approximately 10.42% were Black/African-American, 14.36 Hispanic, 51.41 White non-Hispanic, and 8.31% Asian.

The variable of X3T1CREDCALC indicates that one Carnegie Unit was earned the subject of calculus for a one-year academic course offered one period a day for five days. Approximately 14.72% of the students earned credit and 78.58% did not earn credit, and 6.7% did not have a response.

## Chapter 4

## FINDINGS/RESULTS

This research study was conducted to determine the correlational and predictive role parental education has on a child's earning of credit in high school calculus based on the data from the U.S. Department of Education's 2009 Longitudinal study. The original data file contained 23,504 participants; however, the researcher eliminated those observations where responses were missing. After the missing values were extracted from the dataset, the researcher was left with 18,992 datapoints associated with the variables selected for this study.

This study analyzed two research questions: 1) whether a parent's higher level of education increased the likelihood that his/her child will take and pass calculus in high school, and 2) if a mother's education level was a greater predictor of a child taking high school calculus than the father's education level. Information gathered from the literature review indicated that factors may exist in which the education of the parent influences the education of the child (Sommer, Chase-Lansdale, Brooks-Gunn, Gardner, Rauner, & Freel, 2012).

Hypothesis 1

The first hypothesis examined whether a parent's higher level of education increases the likelihood of passing Calculus.

Table 5.        Levene's Test

| Levene Test | | | | |
| --- | --- | --- | --- | --- |
| Variable A | Variable B | F-value | Df | Significance |
| Calculus credit earned | Parent's Education | 957.04 | 6 | p-value <2.2e-16 |

The Levene's Test looked for Homogeneity of Variance with the F-value being 957.04 and with a probability smaller than 0.001 demonstrating a significance result.

Table 6.    Pearson's Chi-squared Test

| Pearson's Chi-squared Test | | | | |
| --- | --- | --- | --- | --- |
| Variable A | Variable B | X-squared | Df | Significance |
| Calculus credit earned | Parent's Education | 1547.4 | 6 | p-value <2.2e-16 |

The Pearson Chi-squared test measures goodness of fit and tests the null hypothesis. With a p-<.001, the null hypothesis is rejected. The parent's education has a significant effect on whether a child will take calculus in high school and earn credit.

Table 7.    Pearson's Product-Moment Correlation

| Pearson's Product-Moment Correlation | | | | | |
| --- | --- | --- | --- | --- | --- |
| Variable A | Variable B | R | t | Df | Significance |
| Calculus credit earned | Parent's Education | 0.19595 | 37.444 | 18920 | p-value <2.2e-16 |

## Hypothesis 2

The second hypothesis examined whether a mother's education was a better predictor of passing calculus than the father's education.

Table 8.  Simple regression.

| Simple regression | | | | | |
| --- | --- | --- | --- | --- | --- |
| Variable 1 | Variable 2 | Sum Sq. | Df | F Value | Probability |
| Calculus credit earned | Mother's Education | 133.14 | 1 | 989.06 | p- value <2.2e-16 |
| Calculus credit earned | Father's Education | 180.43 | 1 | 1365.8 | p- value <2.2e-16 |

Based upon data from the simple regressions, both the mother's and father's education had a significant result. The father's education had a higher F value than the mother's. When an F test was conducted using the var.test command to compare two variances of mother's education and calculus credit earned to father's education and calculus credit earned, the variance were not equal to one, so the null hypothesis cannot be rejected. A father's education attainment is a better predictor of a child earning credit in college than the mother's educational attainment.

## F-Test

```
> var.test(MomEdX3T1CREDCALC,DadEdX3T1CREDCALC)

        F test to compare two variances

data:  MomEdX3T1CREDCALC and DadEdX3T1CREDCALC
F = 1.0189, num df = 18920, denom df = 18920, p-value = 0.1974
alternative hypothesis: true ratio of variances is not equal to 1
95 percent confidence interval:
 0.9902924 1.0483768
sample estimates:
ratio of variances
        1.018921
```

## Plots

The Q-Q theoretical plots of mother's education and father's education in relation to earning of college credit in high school showed great similarities, but the father's education slope line was slightly higher with different numerical values.

Figure 16.

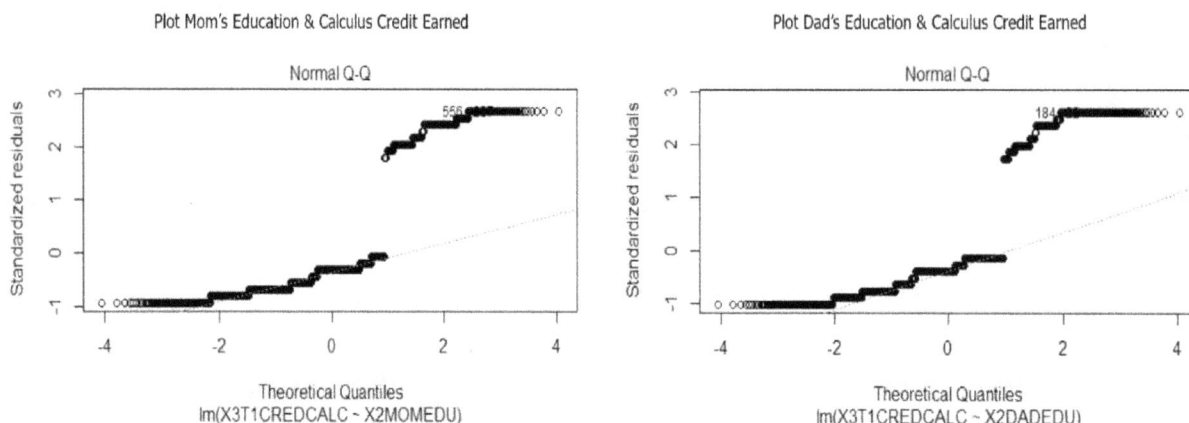

The residuals vs. leverage plot showed differences in the standardized residuals with the trend lines moving in different directions.

Figure 17.

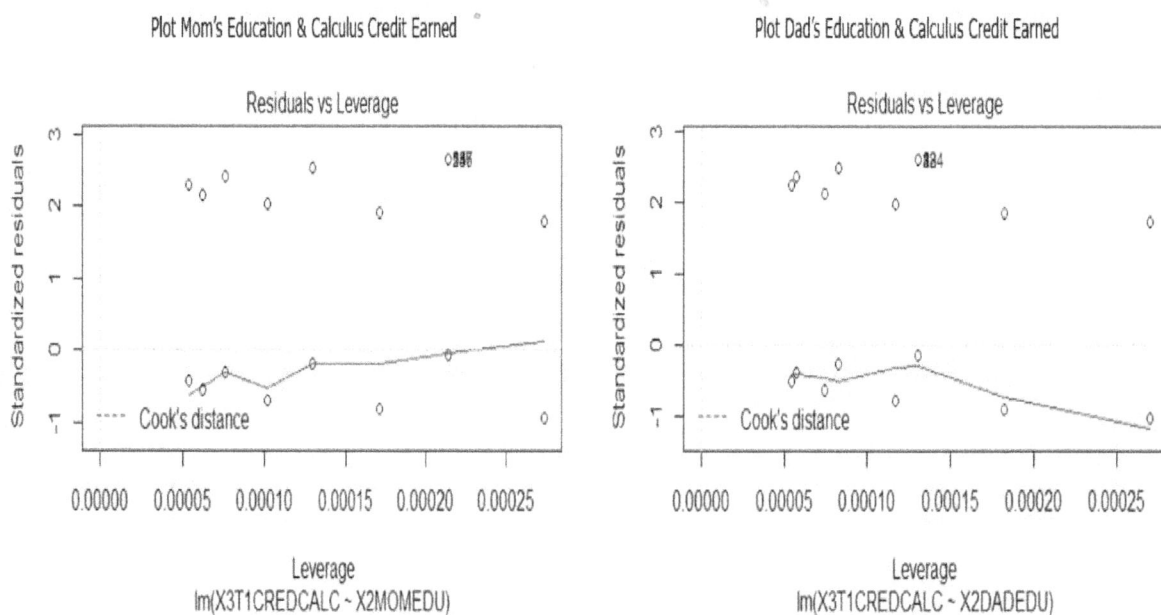

The predictor command was used to make predictions regarding the attainment of calculus credit in high school based upon the mother's and father's education.

Figure 18.

| | Prediction Mom's Education | | |
|---|---|---|---|
| | > predict(MomEdX3T1CREDCALC, interval = 'confidence') | | |
| | fit | lwr | upr |
| 1 | 0.29669489 | 0.28726665 | 0.30612313 |
| 2 | 0.20593416 | 0.20026630 | 0.21160202 |
| 3 | 0.34207525 | 0.33018938 | 0.35396112 |
| 4 | 0.11517343 | 0.10890017 | 0.12144670 |
| 5 | 0.25131452 | 0.24406824 | 0.25856080 |
| 6 | 0.20593416 | 0.20026630 | 0.21160202 |
| 7 | 0.11517343 | 0.10890017 | 0.12144670 |
| 8 | 0.29669489 | 0.28726665 | 0.30612313 |
| 9 | 0.11517343 | 0.10890017 | 0.12144670 |
| 10 | 0.20593416 | 0.20026630 | 0.21160202 |
| 11 | 0.29669489 | 0.28726665 | 0.30612313 |
| 12 | 0.34207525 | 0.33018938 | 0.35396112 |
| 13 | 0.34207525 | 0.33018938 | 0.35396112 |
| 14 | 0.25131452 | 0.24406824 | 0.25856080 |
| 15 | 0.20593416 | 0.20026630 | 0.21160202 |
| 16 | 0.25131452 | 0.24406824 | 0.25856080 |
| 17 | 0.11517343 | 0.10890017 | 0.12144670 |
| 18 | 0.11517343 | 0.10890017 | 0.12144670 |
| 19 | 0.16055380 | 0.15528695 | 0.16582064 |
| 20 | 0.29669489 | 0.28726665 | 0.30612313 |
| 21 | 0.29669489 | 0.28726665 | 0.30612313 |

| | Prediction Dad's Education | | |
|---|---|---|---|
| | > predict(DadEdX3T1CREDCALC, interval = 'confidence') | | |
| | fit | lwr | upr |
| 1 | 0.32348469 | 0.31387230 | 0.33309708 |
| 2 | 0.14254477 | 0.13715304 | 0.14793649 |
| 3 | 0.05207480 | 0.04392127 | 0.06022834 |
| 4 | 0.23301473 | 0.22687388 | 0.23915558 |
| 5 | 0.05207480 | 0.04392127 | 0.06022834 |
| 6 | 0.27824971 | 0.27054919 | 0.28595023 |
| 7 | 0.14254477 | 0.13715304 | 0.14793649 |
| 8 | 0.05207480 | 0.04392127 | 0.06022834 |
| 9 | 0.18777975 | 0.18252292 | 0.19303658 |
| 10 | 0.18777975 | 0.18252292 | 0.19303658 |
| 11 | 0.23301473 | 0.22687388 | 0.23915558 |
| 12 | 0.36871967 | 0.35701453 | 0.38042482 |
| 13 | 0.36871967 | 0.35701453 | 0.38042482 |
| 14 | 0.27824971 | 0.27054919 | 0.28595023 |
| 15 | 0.14254477 | 0.13715304 | 0.14793649 |
| 16 | 0.36871967 | 0.35701453 | 0.38042482 |
| 17 | 0.14254477 | 0.13715304 | 0.14793649 |
| 18 | 0.23301473 | 0.22687388 | 0.23915558 |
| 19 | 0.14254477 | 0.13715304 | 0.14793649 |
| 20 | 0.32348469 | 0.31387230 | 0.33309708 |
| 21 | 0.23301473 | 0.22687388 | 0.23915558 |

When the qplot was generated for the mother's and father's predictive educational attainment, there were similarities between the tail end of the plot, but the father's overall range was slightly higher.

Figure 19.

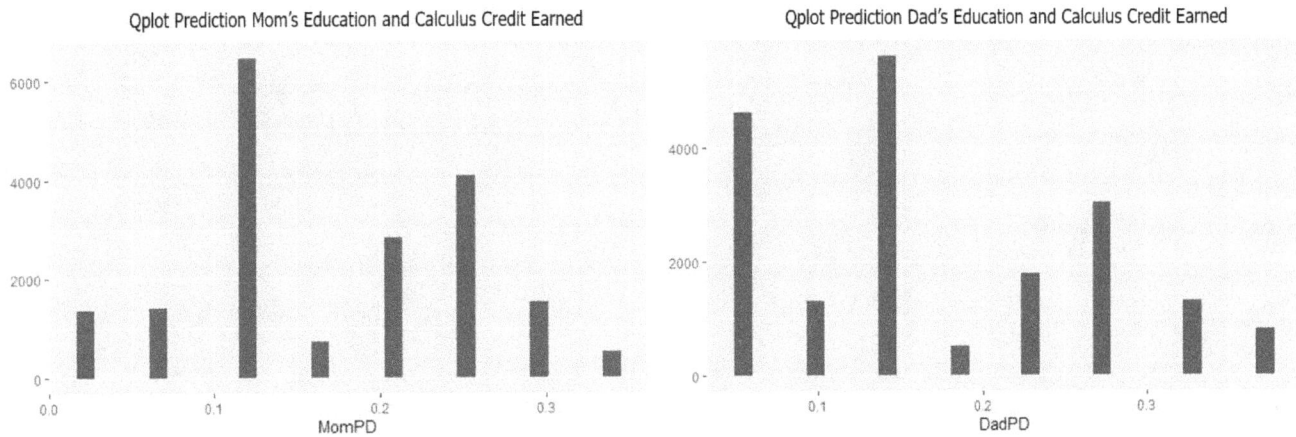

Qplot Prediction Mom's Education and Calculus Credit Earned

Qplot Prediction Dad's Education and Calculus Credit Earned

An F-test was conducted using the var.test to compare the predictive model of mother's educational attainment and father's educational attainment in relation to their child earning calculus credit in high school. The variances were not equal to 1. The null hypothesis was rejected. The father's educational attainment was a better predictor of a child earning credit in high school for calculus than the mother's.

```
> var.test(MomPD,DadPD)

        F test to compare two variances

data:  MomPD and DadPD
F = 0.73789, num df = 18921, denom df = 18921, p-value < 2.2e-16
alternative hypothesis: true ratio of variances is not equal to 1
95 percent confidence interval:
 0.7171558 0.7592186
sample estimates:
ratio of variances
        0.7378876
```

**Chapter 5**

**DISCUSSION**

Over the past decade, a dramatic decline in the percentage of U.S. born citizens graduating with a STEM college degree has threatened the technological dominance of the nation (NSB, 2003; NSB, 2016; NSF, 2018). Although dominance in STEM participation in and of itself is not a goal per se, the recent trajectory is evidence that the overall number of participations in STEM careers across the nation continues to decline as compared to the participation of citizens of many other countries in the world. The majority of graduate level engineering degrees in the U.S. are earned by foreign born individuals (Redden, 2017). Additionally, a global gender paradox exists in which the more advanced that a nation becomes, the less likely that it is for a woman to graduate with a STEM degree (World Economic Forum, 2018). The overly aggressive masculine workplace culture of men is a source of one deterrent for women seeking STEM careers (Cheryan, Ziegler, Montoya, & Jiang, 2017). Other factors affecting STEM participation may originate from parental human capital investments. A correlation exists between the monetary human capital potential of the parents and their investments into the education of their children (Becker & Tomes, 1985). Moreover, underrepresented minorities tend to earn less per capita than their other racial counterparts resulting in less money being invested in the education development of their children (Becker & Tomes, 1985). Deindustrialization and high unemployment are just two documented factors, among many others, contributing to the destabilization of family structures (Lipsitz, 1998).

African Americans are more likely to be born into poverty (Winship, Reeves, & Guyot, 2018), and African American women earn 60% of the college degrees awarded to African-Americans creating an educational gap within the group (Mcdaniel, Diprete, Buchmann, &

Shwed, 2011). Intergenerational poverty within the African American community is strongly influenced by the economic productivity of the African American males (Winship, Reeves, & Guyot, 2018). Educated African-American women tend to marry at a lower rate (Mcdaniel, Diprete, Buchmann, & Shwed, 2011). The long-term consequence of educated African-American women remaining unmarried and raising children as single mothers may result in intergenerational poverty perpetuation and hardship. The poverty rate for single African-American mothers is 30% (Duffin, 2019). The greater the household income, the more that parents tend to invest in their children (Becker, & Tomes, 1994).

Educational attainment remains a challenge in both the Hispanic and African American communities. According to the DOE, students who took calculus in high school had the lowest attrition rate in college (DOE, 2014). This conclusion is interpret to mean that access to calculus in high school together with the aptitude to do well in the course are strong predictors of college success. Hispanics and African Americans are less likely to take high school calculus in comparison to their Caucasian and Asian American counterparts (DOE, 2014; NSB, 2016). Some of the reasons associated with these trends are factors such as variable availability of calculus courses in the schools, with lowest or no availability seen in the schools with lower ratings, as well as level of preparedness of the students associated with inclination to take calculus when it is offered and ability to successfully pass the course when it is offered. Furthermore, in a study conducted by Tyson (2011), it was found that for students in the state of Florida, as an example, the greatest predictor of whether an individual earned a STEM degree in the future was whether or not the student took and earned calculus credit in high school. The direct link between the two offers one approach to possible interventions which can be used to mediate the current trajectory for the U.S. of declining participation in STEM careers. School districts can invest more resources in addressing the needs of the students in regards to the crucial role of calculus in high school. Pilot programs can be designed to build on the validity of the conclusions made in regards to calculus courses in high schools and to measure the effect of those programs across many types of school districts and understand student outcomes.

In the current study, it was found that one of the greatest predictors of a student taking calculus in high school was the educational attainment of the parent based upon cumulative test results from the Pearson Chi-square test, the Pearson's Product-Moment correlations, and regressions. The educational attainment of the father was more statistically significant than the mother. Further research is necessary to investigate what elements of parental education level, whether father's, mother's or both, are contributing the greatest impact to this finding. For example, one question to explore is whether the major the parent/s pursued has a differential effect. Another question to consider is the role of the career path the parent took and whether the career path is actually directly related to the major the parent pursued during his/her education – so if a parent is a nurse, does it matter significantly whether that parent stopped education at a bachelor, master, or doctoral level. Another question to consider is whether the parental high level of education is associated with a particular threshold of financial resources. For instance, even though a parent can hold a doctoral degree, the chosen field of study may not have led to a particularly high income, and thus availability of financial resources that can be invested in the educational attainment of children within the family.

Post-Hoc Analyses

While total level of parental education as well as the mother's and father's level of education were found to be significantly associated with a child taking calculus in high school, the role of race and gender were also explored in the current sample. As was predicted based on the current literature, race was statistically significant as to whether a child did or did not earn calculus in high school; however, gender was not significant (Table 8). One possible reason that gender was not a significant factor, a finding that goes against current literature, is that the construct of cultural masculinity is applicable for the workforce of adults but it may not necessarily be appropriate to high school students.

Table 8.

**Pearson's Chi-squared Test**

| Variable A | Variable B | X-squared | Df | P-value |
|---|---|---|---|---|
| **Calculus credit earned** | Parent's Education | 1547.4 | 6 | <2.2e-16 |
| **Calculus credit earned** | Mother's Education | 1168.8 | 7 | <2.2e-16 |
| **Calculus credit earned** | Father's Education | 1658.1 | 7 | <2.2e-16 |
| **Calculus credit earned** | Race | 1128.7 | 7 | <2.2e-16 |
| **Calculus credit earned** | Gender | 0.56867 | 1 | 0.4508 |

One of the post-hoc analyses in this study included an investigation of the relations of the parent's education to child taking calculus in high school. Through the analysis of the DOE variable of X2PAREDU, it was found that only 8.54% of students whose parents had a high school diploma earned calculus credit as compared to 44.08% of students whose parents earned a doctoral degree (Table 9). First-generation students were less likely to have taken calculus in high school.

**Table 9.**

| # | Highest level of Parent's education | Population | Students that earned calculus credit | Percentage of students earned calculus credit |
|---|---|---|---|---|
| 1 | No high school diploma | 981 | 59 | 6.01% |
| 2 | High school diploma | 5783 | 494 | 8.54% |
| 3 | Certificate/diploma (trade school) | 896 | 63 | 7.03% |
| 4 | Associates degree | 3009 | 327 | 10.87% |
| 5 | Bachelor's degree | 4666 | 1021 | 21.88% |
| 6 | Master's degree | 2380 | 736 | 30.92% |
| 7 | Doctorate | 1207 | 532 | 44.08% |
| | **TOTAL** | 18922 | 3232 | |

There are many variables related to a student having access to calculus, passing the course, and selecting a STEM major from a four-year university. These factors include but are not limited to: household income (SES), race, the employment status of the father, and the employment status of the mother. SES ties directly into a parent's ability to invest capital into the educational attainment of his/her child (Odgers & Adler, 2018). College-educated individuals earn more money throughout their lifetime than non-college-graduates (Torpey, 2018). Education is associated with opportunities. Intergenerational poverty and access to financial resources should remain an ongoing area of study considering their pervasive nature on familial cycles and the ability to withstand the effects of those cycles. Additionally, supportive environments may increase the academic self-determination of disenfranchised students (Paixão & Gamboa, 2017). Future research should continue to explore this topic. For instance, significant attention needs to be devoted to interventions that can be especially effective for those students at the greatest disadvantages (presence of multiple negative factors simultaneously such as low SES, low educational attainment of parents, family unit structure, etc.).

One may argue that increasing access to calculus alone may not be the panacea for improving the probability of a child graduating from college and even moving into a STEM career. The current study's data indicates that a parent's education is one of the significant predictors of a student earning calculus credit; however, there may be many other factors that have a significant relationship on taking calculus. This research gives light to one lens deciphering the cycle of educational attainment illustrating that college-educated parents tend to have college-educated children. Other potential factors may be just as powerful or more powerful in explaining the association with engagement with high school calculus.

According to the NSF (2017), 69% of all doctoral STEM recipients had at least one parent who earned a doctorate. In the current research, 44% of children who had parents with doctoral degrees took and passed calculus in high school in comparison with a mere 8.54% of children whose parents only obtained a high school diploma. Future research is needed to better understand the environmental, socio-economic, and psychological factors that will propel students most vulnerable, for example first-generation college students, Hispanic and African American students, female students, to greater levels of academic success within the STEM fields. Additionally, questions remain regarding the development of programs to academically accelerate at-risk underrepresented minority students at an early age.

### Recommendations

The results of this study indicate that parental education plays a significant role in determining the high school calculus completion rate of a child (Bainbridge, Meyers, Tanaka, & Waldfogel, 2005; Barshay, 2015). As the parent's educational attainment increases, the likelihood of the child passing calculus in high school increases. For a variety of reasons, parents of children within underrepresented communities may not choose to go back to school to further their education even when given an opportunity. In the African American community, 51.1% of all households are headed by unmarried single mothers (Glynn, 2019), so going back to school would mean that the mother would spend less quality time with her children. Therefore, to close the mathematical achievement gap, several different approaches should be taken to accelerate the success of a child. In the section below, a proposal for two pilot programs for closing the mathematics achievement gap is suggested as one approach to the practical application of the current study.

Pilot Program Summer School

The majority of students entering high school within the Chicago Public School System begin their mathematical studies at the level of algebra 1. In their sophomore year, they take geometry, followed by algebra II/trigonometry in their junior year. Some students may opt-out of taking a fourth year of mathematics.

A summer school pilot program could be started with a cohort of underrepresented minorities. In this program, freshmen students enrolled in algebra would be incentivized to take geometry in the summer months with a monetary stipend based upon attendance and successful completion of the course. A summer stipend would create a tangible positive goal while reinforcing positive psychology regarding math. The program can include breakfast and lunch since students will be away from home for an extended time frame. When the students return to school in their sophomore year, they will begin the year at the level of algebra II/trigonometry. In the summer of their sophomore year, students would take college algebra and receive a slightly larger stipend. When they returned to school in their junior year, they would take pre-calculus. It is anticipated that when participating students would take the ACT and/or SAT, they would likely score higher on the mathematics portion of the test as compared to likely scores without participating in the pilot math program. Students would be strongly encouraged to take AP calculus their senior year. The monetary incentive along with mentoring would motivate students to overcome any psychological bias that they or their parents may have toward STEM (Mervis, 2014).

For several years, Richard T. Crane High School, on the Westside of Chicago has provided opportunities for students to join the Schuler program. Students enrolled in the Schuler program take geometry the summer before their sophomore year if they began their freshman year at the level of algebra. The Schuler program has assisted more than 1,200 first-generation students and underrepresented minorities in Chicago with preparing and going to college (Schuler, 2019). The Schuler program has partnerships with four Chicago Public schools, George Westinghouse College Prep, Lindblom, Gwendolyn Brooks College Preparatory Academy, and Richard T. Crane Medical Preparatory High School (Schuler, 2019). The success of the Schuler program validates the need for similar programs.

## The Genesis of a City-Wide Program

A large school district like the Chicago Board of Education (CBOE) could form a Mathematical Achievement Gap Think Tank to review relevant research. The collaborative could create two pilot programs with one being aimed at elementary schools and the other at high schools. Next, the CBOE could send letters, emails, or calls to the homes of 350 underrepresented freshmen high school students' families who are currently earning a B or better in algebra 1. Interested parents would attend a mandatory two-hour orientation. There would be greeters at the door to meet the parents as they entered the building to provide directions. The hallway would contain tables for parents to sign in electronically and by hand. The session would begin with a welcome from a leader from the Chicago Public Schools and a school principal. A presenter would share a short research study communicating the value-add in taking calculus before a student leaves high school, then the pilot program would be discussed. The students participating in the pilot would be paid through direct deposit to a bank account in two installments. The first installment would occur at the 50% mark and the final installment when they complete the program. Each class would contain at least two teachers, and the class size would not exceed 15 students. In this model, a school system such as the Chicago Board of Education would need to recruit 40 math teachers for the summer pilot. The teachers would be paid their normal summer school salary along with a stipend of $1,200.

The summer program would begin with an orientation of the students in the main auditorium. The students would meet the teachers, receive t-shirts and a schedule, learn about the overall expectations, engage in a 'fun ice-breaker', and take a brief 15 question math pre-test. Every student would receive a book bag containing a scientific calculator, a composition notebook, a folder, three pencils, and a formula sheet. Each class would begin with a 'bell-ringer' or 'do now' which is a short math problem that could be completed in seven minutes. The students would use a formula sheet to find the values of geometric shapes using algebra skills. Once a student solved the problem, he/she would be invited to work out the problem on the board. Students would be required to record the problem in their notebooks.

Pilot Program Mathematics Integration

In the city of Chicago, most students do not receive a stand-alone math teacher until the 7th grade. From K-6th grade, one teacher provides instruction in all subjects even if the teacher may not be proficient in mathematics. Based on the results of the current study, it is proposed for large school districts to launch a pilot program at two elementary schools that would allow students to receive a stand-alone math teacher beginning in the fourth grade. Teachers would see the students for 90 minutes per day Monday-Friday. Classes would begin with a brief 'bell ringer' or 'do now'. The regular teacher would be expected to remain in the classroom during math instruction to assist with classroom management. Students would receive a pre-test at the beginning of the year and post-test at the end. The student test results from the two pilot elementary schools would be compared against schools with similar demographics over two years to determine whether a statistical difference exists in mathematical achievement between the pilot schools and non-pilot schools. During the pilot program, the regular teacher that has been assigned to the classroom should not see a drop in the salary as a result of another teacher providing instruction in mathematics. Teachers would be strongly encouraged to give students timed assignments and allow students to engage in reciprocal teaching by encouraging the strongest students to work out problems on the board in front of their peers. In the future, municipalities and local governments could take major steps through educational initiatives and pilot programs to close the mathematics achievement gap and positively transform lives.

## Future Research Hypothesis

The research study of *Minority Students in STEM Careers in the U.S. – the Role of AP Calculus* may lead to the exploration of other longitudinal questions such as: what are the long-term benefits of offering a monetary incentive for underrepresented minorities to take mathematics during the summer months. Future research efforts could explore many potential hypotheses. One example is the exploration of whether First-generation underrepresented minorities who take high school calculus graduate from high school and college at the same rate as their peers.

**Ramifications to Higher Education**

Research conducted by the DOE demonstrated that students who graduated from high school at the level of calculus and expressed an interest in STEM had a lower college attrition rate (DOE, 2014). The Cleveland Federal Reserve Bank indicated that students who took advanced mathematics in high school earned more money throughout their life-time (James, 2013; Thompson, 2013). Higher education recruitment officers may attempt to increase the overall graduation rate of their student body by recruiting more students who advanced mathematics in high school. Additionally, higher education institutions should work closely with their top feeder high schools through strategic investments to ensure that more of the students graduate at the level of calculus. Colleges and universities can continue to build partnerships with local high schools to offer programs like summer math camps and remedial math preparation courses to help high school students be more prepared for college-level math expectations as well as connect students' aspirations to attainable educational pathways. More work must be invested in this area to support the national needs for STEM career participation, especially as it relates to underrepresented students.

References

ACOLA (2013). STEM country comparison. *Australian Academy of Science*. Retrieved from

https://acola.org.au/wp/PDF/SAF02Consultants/SAF02_STEM_%20FINAL.pdf

Adams, R. (2014). Father's education level strongest factor in child's success at school. *The*

*Guardian.* Retrieved from https://www.theguardian.com/society/2014/sep/23/fathers-

education-child-success-school

Akee, R., Jones, M. R., & Porter, S. R. (2019). Race matters: Income shares, income inequality,

and income mobility for all U.S. races. *Demography,* 1-23.

doi:http://dx.doi.org.nl.idm.oclc.org/10.1007/s13524-019-00773-7

Bainbridge, J., Meyers, M. K., Tanaka, S., & Waldfogel, J. (2005). Who gets an early education?

family income and the enrollment of three- to five-year-olds from 1968 to 2000. *Social*

*Science Quarterly, 86*(3), 724-745.

Barshay, J. (2015). Signs that few black students are taking calculus in high school. *Hechinger*

*Report.* Retrieved from https://hechingerreport.org/signs-that-fewer-black-students-are-

taking-calculus-in-high-school/

Battey, D. (2013). Access to Mathematics: A Possessive investment in whiteness. *Curriculum*

*Inquiry, 43*(3), 332–359. https://doi-org.nl.idm.oclc.org/10.1111/curi.12015

Becker, G. & Tomes, N. (1985). *Human Capital: A theoretical and empirical analysis with*

*special reference to education* (3rd Edition).

Bloome, D. (2017). Childhood family structure and intergenerational income mobility in the

United States. *Demography. 54*(2). 541-569.

Bloome, D. (2014). Racial Inequality Trends and the Intergenerational Persistence of Income and

Family Structure. *American Sociological Review, 79*(6), 1196–1225. https://doi-

org.nl.idm.oclc.org/10.1177/0003122414554947

BLS (2019). Table A-2. Employment status of civilian population by race, sex, and age.

*U.S. Department of Labor: Bureau of Labor Statistics.* Retrieved from

https://www.bls.gov/news.release/empsit.t02.htm

Bolick, C. (2017). Jump-starting K-12 education reform. *Harvard Journal of Law and Public

Policy, 40*(1), 17-24.

Byun, S., Irvin, M. J., & Bell, B. A. (2015). Advanced math course taking: Effects on math

achievement and college enrollment. *Journal of Experimental Education, 83*(4), 439–

468. https://doi-org.nl.idm.oclc.org/10.1080/00220973.2014.919570

Cheryan, S., Ziegler, S. A., Montoya, A. K., & Jiang, L. (2017). Why are some STEM fields

more gender-balanced than others? *Psychological Bulletin, 143*(1), 1.

James, J. (2013). The surprising impact of high school math on job market outcomes. Federal

Reserve Bank of Cleveland. Retrieved from https://www.clevelandfed.org/newsroom-

and-events/publications/economic-commentary/2013-economic-commentaries/ec-

201314-the-surprising-impact-of-high-school-math-on-job-market-outcomes.aspx

Cohen, L. & Rubinsten, (2017). Mothers, intrinsic math motivation, arithmetic skills, and math

anxiety in elementary school. *Frontiers in Psychology.*, 8, doi: 10.3389/fpsyg.2017.01939

CRDC (2015). U.S. Department of Education Office for Civil Rights. Civil Rights Data

Collection. Retrieved from https://ocrdata.ed.gov/flex/Reports.aspx?type=school

Dickerson, K. (2013). 'I'm not a math person' is no longer a valid excuse. *Business Insider,*

https://www.businessinsider.com/being-good-at-math-is-not-about-natural-ability-2013-

11

Diemer, M. A. & Ali, S. R. (2009). Integrating social class into vocational psychology: Theory

and practice implications. *Journal of Career Assessment, 17,* 247-265.

doi:10.1177/1069072708330462

DOE (2014). U.S. Department of Education, National Center for Education Statistics, STEM

attrition: College students' paths into and out of STEM fields. Retrieved June 2, 2018,

from https://nces.ed.gov/pubs2014/2014001rev.pdf

DOE (2012). U.S. Department of Education, Web tables, STEM in postsecondary education:

Entrance, attrition, and course taking among 2003 – 2004 beginning postsecondary

students.

Doerschuk, P., Bahrim, C., Daniel, J., Kruger, J., Mann, J., & Martin, C. (2016). Closing the

gaps and filling the STEM pipeline: A multidisciplinary approach. *Journal of Science*

*Education and Technology, 25,* 682-695. doi:10.1007/s10956-016-9622-8

Duffin, E. (2019). Poverty rate of Black families with single mother in the U.S. 1990 to 2017.

*Statista.* Received from https://www.statista.com/statistics/205114/percentage-of-poor-

black-families-with-a-female-householder-in-the-us/

Estudillo-Martínez, M. D., Castillo-Gutiérrez, S., & Lozano-Aguilera, E. D. (2013). New

confidence bands in Q–Q Plots to detect non-normality. *International Journal of*

*Computer Mathematics, 90*(10), 2137–2146. https://doi-

org.nl.idm.oclc.org/10.1080/00207160.2013.792920

Funk, C. & Parker, K. (2018). Blacks in STEM jobs are especially concerned about diversity and

    discrimination in the workplace. *Pew Research Center.* Retrieved from

    https://www.pewsocialtrends.org/2018/01/09/blacks-in-stem-jobs-are-especially-

    concerned-about-diversity-and-discrimination-in-the-workplace/

Garraghan, G. (1983). *The Jesuits of the middle United States.* Chicago: Loyola University Press

Gastwirth, J. L. (2014). Median-based measures of inequality: Reassessing the increase in

    income inequality in the U.S. and Sweden. Statistical Journal of the IAOS, 30(4), 311–

    320. https://doi-org.nl.idm.oclc.org/10.3233/SJI-140842

Glynn, S. (2019). Breadwinning mothers continue to be the U.S. norm. Center for American

    Progress. Retrieved from

    https://www.americanprogress.org/issues/women/reports/2019/05/10/469739/breadwinni

    ng-mothers-continue-u-s-norm/

Hansmann, H. (2012). The evolving economic structure of higher education. *The University of*

    *Chicago Law Review, 79*(1), 161-185.

Jeno, L. M., Danielsen, A. G., & Raaheim, A. (2018). A prospective investigation of students'

    academic achievement and dropout in higher education: a Self-Determination Theory

    approach. *Educational Psychology, 38*(9), 1163–1184. https://doi-

    org.nl.idm.oclc.org/10.1080/01443410.2018.1502412

Jost, A. (2017). SLU medical school put on probation by an accreditation agency. *St. Louis*

    *Post-Dispatch.* Retrieved from June 10, 2018, from

    https://www.stltoday.com/opinion/columnists/slu-school-of-medicine-on-

    probation/article_1e873daa-cce7-50b8-84da-b93858fd76a2.html

Hao, L., & Yeung, W.-J. (2015). Parental Spending on School-Age Children: Structural Stratification and Parental Expectation. *Demography, 52*(3), 835–860. https://doi-org.nl.idm.oclc.org/10.1007/s13524-015-0386-1

Karuguti, W. M., Phillips, J., & Barr, H. (2017). Analyzing the cognitive rigor of interprofessional curriculum using the Depth of Knowledge framework. *Journal of Interprofessional Care, 31*(4), 529–532. https://doi-org.nl.idm.oclc.org/10.1080/13561820.2017.1310718

Kim, J., Chatterjee, S., Young, J., & Moon, U. J. (2017). The cost of access: Racial disparities in student loan burdens of young adults. *College Student Journal, 51*(1), 99-114.

Kochan, T., Finegold, D., & Osterman, P. (2012). Who can fix the "middle skills" gap? *Harvard Business Review, 90*, 82-90.

LCME (2017). Saint Louis University full survey. Liaison Committee on Medical Education. Retrieved June 10, 2018, from https://www.slu.edu/_resources/widgets/lcme/lcme-letter.pdf

Li, S. (2018). From 985 to World Class 2.0: China's Strategic Move. *Inside Higher Ed*. Retrieved from https://www.insidehighered.com/blogs/world-view/985-world-class-20-chinas-strategic-move

Lipsitz, G. (2016). *Possessive investment in whiteness. How White people profit from identify politic*s. Philadelphia: Temple University Press

Lopez, G., Ruiz, N., & Patten, E. (2017). Key Facts about Asian American's diverse and growing population. Pew Research Center. Retrieved from https://www.pewresearch.org/fact-tank/2017/09/08/key-facts-about-asian-americans/

MacQueen, K. M., McLellan, E., Metzger, D.S, Kegeles, S., Strauss, R.P, Scotti, R, Blanchard,

    L., & Trotter, R. (2001). *American Journal of Public Health,* 91(12): 1929-38

Marcus, J. (2017). Why men are the new college minority. *The Atlantic.* Retrieved from

    https://www.theatlantic.com/education/archive/2017/08/why-men-are-the-new-college-

    minority/536103/

Mcdaniel, A., Diprete, T. A., Buchmann, C., & Shwed, U. (2011). The black gender gap in

    educational attainment: Historical trends and racial comparisons. *Demography, 48*(3),

    889-914. doi:http://dx.doi.org.nl.idm.oclc.org/10.1007/s13524-011-0037-0

Mervis, J. (2014). Summer jobs lower violent-crime rate for urban teen. *Science Magazine.*

    346(6214), pg. 1219-1223, DOI: 10.1126/science.1257809, Retrieved from

    https://www.sciencemag.org/news/2014/12/summer-jobs-lower-violent-crime-rate-urban-

    teens

NAEP (2017). National achievement-level results. The Nations Report Card. Retrieved from

    https://www.nationsreportcard.gov/math_2017/nation/achievement?grade=4

National Science Board (2003). The science and engineering workforce: Realizing America's

    potential. NSB 03-69. Retrieved from

    http://www.nsf.gov/nsb/documents/2003/nsb0369/nsb0369.pdf

NSB (2012). Science and Engineering Indicators 2012. Retrieved from

    https://files.eric.ed.gov/fulltext/ED528689.pdf

NSB (2016). Science and Engineering Indicators 2016. Retrieved from

    https://www.nsf.gov/nsb/publications/2016/nsb20161.pdf

NSF (2017). 2015 doctorate recipients from U.S. universities. National Science Foundation.

    https://www.nsf.gov/statistics/2017/nsf17306/static/report/nsf17306.pdf

NSF (2018). Graduate education enrollment degrees in the United States. National Science

    Foundation. Retrieved from

    https://www.nsf.gov/statistics/2018/nsb20181/report/sections/higher-education-in-

    science-and-engineering/graduate-education-enrollment-and-degrees-in-the-united-states

NSF (2018). National Science Foundation, National Center for Science and Engineering

    Statistics, special tabulations (2016) of high school longitudinal study of 2009

    (HSLS:09), National Center for Education Statistics. Retrieved from

    https://www.nsf.gov/statistics/2018/nsb20181/report/sections/elementary-and-secondary-

    mathematics-and-science-education/high-school-coursetaking-in-mathematics-and-

    science#demographic-differences-in-access-to-advanced-mathematics-and-science-

    courses-civil-rights-data

NSF (2018). The rise of China in science and engineering. National Science Board. Retrieved

    from https://nsf.gov/nsb/sei/one-pagers/China-2018.pdf

Odgers, C. L., & Adler, N. E. (2018). Challenges for low-income children in an era of increasing

    income inequality. *Child Development Perspectives, 12*(2), 128–133. https://doi-

    org.nl.idm.oclc.org/10.1111/cdep.12273

Paixão, O. & Gamboa, V. (2017). Motivational Profiles and Career Decision Making of High

    School Students. *Career Development Quarterly, 65*(3), 207–221. https://doi-

    org.nl.idm.oclc.org/10.1002/cdq.12093

Perna, L., May, H., Yee, A., Ransom, T., Rodriguez, A., & Fester, R. (2015). Unequal access to

    rigorous high school curricula: An exploration of the opportunity to benefit from the

    international baccalaureate diploma programme. *Educational Policy, 29(2), 400-425.*

    *Retrieved from* https://eric.ed.gov/?id=EJ1054288

Petrin, K. (2017). How a chimpanzee attack inspired the Andrew Oberle to found a SLU trauma

    care program. *St. Louis Magazine*. Retrieved from

    https://www.stlmag.com/health/news/how-a-chimpanzee-attack-inspired-andrew-oberle-

    to-found-a-tr/

Pew (2018). Diversity in the STEM workforce varies widely across jobs. *Pew Research Center*.

    Retrieved from https://www.pewsocialtrends.org/2018/01/09/diversity-in-the-stem-

    workforce-varies-widely-across-jobs/

Pew (2019). Sampling methods. *Pew Research Center*. Retrieved from

    https://www.pewresearch.org/methods/u-s-survey-research/our-survey-methodology-in-

    detail/

PISA (2015). Mathematics literacy: Proficiency levels. *Program for International Student*

    *Assessment*. Retrieved from

    https://nces.ed.gov/surveys/pisa/pisa2015/pisa2015highlights_5a.asp

Ployhart, R. E., Nyberg, A. J., Reilly, G., & Maltarich, M. A. (2014). Human capital is dead;

    long live human capital resources! *Journal of Management, 40*(2), 371-398.

Priess-groben, H. & Hyde, J. (2017). Implicit theories, expectations, and values predict

    mathematics motivation and behavior across high school and college. *Journal of Youth*

    *and Adolescence, 46*(6). DOI:10.1007/s10964-016-0579-y

Reardon, S. F., Valentino, R. A., Kalogrides, D., Shores, K. A., & Greenberg, E. H.

    (2013). *Patterns and trends in racial academic achievement gaps among states, 1999-*

    *2011*. Retrieved from https://cepa.stanford.edu/content/patterns-and-trends-racial-

    academic-achievement-gaps-among-states-1999-2011

Redden, E. (2019). International Student Numbers in U.S. decline. Inside Higher Education.

    Retrieved from https://www.insidehighered.com/quicktakes/2019/04/23/international-

    student-numbers-us-decline

Redden, E. (2017). Foreign students and graduate STEM enrollment. *Inside Higher Education.*

    Retrieved from https://www.insidehighered.com/quicktakes/2017/10/11/foreign-students-

    and-graduate-stem-enrollment

Reeves, R. & Rodrigue, E. (2017). The century gap: Low economic mobility war. The Brookings

    Institute. Retrieved from https://www.brookings.edu/research/the-century-gap-low-

    economic-mobility-for-black-men-150-years-after-the-civil-war/

Roesler, S. (2016). State standing to challenge federal authority in the modern administrative

    state. *Washington Law Review, 91*(2), 637-702.

Sanchez, G., Nevarez, T., Schink, W., & Hayes-Bautista. (2015). Latino physicians in the

    United States, 1980 – 2010: A thirty-year overview from the censuses. *Academic*

    *Medicine, 90*(7), 906-912.

Saul, S. (2018). As flow of foreign students wanes, U.S. universities feel the sting. *New York*

    *Times.* Retrieved from https://www.nytimes.com/2018/01/02/us/international-

    enrollment-drop.html

Scott, W., Reeves, R., & Guyot. (2018). The inheritance of black poverty: It's all about the men.

    The Brookings Institute. Retrieved from https://www.brookings.edu/research/the-

    inheritance-of-black-poverty-its-all-about-the-men/

Serino, L. (2017). What international test scores reveal about American education. The

    Brookings Institute. Retrieved from https://www.brookings.edu/blog/brown-center-

    chalkboard/2017/04/07/what-international-test-scores-reveal-about-american-education/

SLU (2019). Office of the President. Retrieved from

   https://www.slu.edu/about/leadership/office-president.php

SLU (2018). Medical Scholar's requirement. Saint Louis University. Retrieved from

   https://www.slu.edu/scholars/pdfs/med-scholar-requirements-oct.pdf

SLU (2018). Mission statement. Saint Louis University. Retrieved from

   https://www.slu.edu/about/catholic-jesuit-identity/mission.php

SLU (2017). SLU's Andrew Oberle Epitomizes Power of Resilience, Tenacity. Saint Louis

   University. Retrieved from https://www.slu.edu/news/2017/october/oberle-institute-

   launches.php

SLU (2015). Factbook 2015-2016. Saint Louis University. Retrieved from

   https://www.slu.edu/provost/office-of-institutional-research/institutional-data/pdfs/2015-

   16-fact-book.pdf

SLU (2015). Magis: Saint Louis University Strategic Plan. Retrieved from

   https://www.slu.edu/about/leadership/docs/magis-september-2015.pdf

Soave, D. & Sun, L. (2017). A generalized Levene's scale test for variance heterogeneity in the

   presence of sample correlation and group uncertainty. *Biometrics, 73*(3), pg. 960-971

Sommer, T. E., Chase-Lansdale, P. L., Brooks-Gunn, J., Gardner, M., Rauner, D. M., & Freel, K.

   (2012). Early Childhood Education Centers and Mothers' Postsecondary Attainment: A

   New Conceptual Framework for a Dual-Generation Education Intervention. *Teachers*

   *College Record, 114*(10), 1–40.

So Yoon, Y. & Strobel, J. (2017). Trends in Texas high school student enrollment in

   mathematics, science, and CTE-STEM courses, *International Journal STEM Education,*

   *4*(1), pg. 9, doi: 10.1186/s40594-017-0063-6

Stack, R. & Meredith, A. (2018). The impact of financial hardship on single parents: An exploration of the journey from social distress to seeking help. *Journal of Family and Economic Issues, 39(2),* pg. 233-242, doi: 10.1007/s10834-017-9551-6

St. Louis College (1904). *Catalogue of the St. Louis University.* St. Louis: Nixon-Jones Printing Co.

Suskie, L. (2014). *Five dimensions of quality: A common sense guide to accreditation and accountability.* San Francisco, CA: Jossey-Bass/Wiley.

Taylor, M. (2013). Shared governance in the modern university. *Higher Education Quarterly, 67*(1), 80-94. doi:10.1111/hequ.12003

Teixeira, P. (2016). Economic beliefs and institutional politics: Human capital theory and the changing views of the World Bank about education (1950–1985). *The European Journal of the History of Economic Thought, 24(3).* https://doi.org/10.1080/09672567.2016.1186205

The Federal Reserve Bank (2019). Identifying opportunities and occupations. Retrieved from https://philadelphiafed.org/-/media/community-development/publications/special-reports/identifying_opportunity_occupations/opportunity_occupations_revisited.pdf?la=en

Thompson, D. (2013). Will studying math make you richer? *The Atlantic.* Retrieved from https://www.theatlantic.com/business/archive/2013/11/will-studying-math-make-you-richer/281104/

Topitzes, J., Godes, O., Mersky, J., Ceglarek, S., & Reynolds, A. (2009). Educational success and adult health: Findings from the Chicago Longitudinal Study. *Prevention Science, 10(*2), 175-195. doi: 10.1007/s11121-009-0121-5

Torpey, E. (2018). Measuring the value of education. *Bureau of Labor Statistics.* Retrieved from

    https://www.bls.gov/careeroutlook/2018/data-on-display/education-pays.htm

Toossi, M. (2002). A century of change: the U.S. labor force, 1950-2050. Labor Force Change.

    *Bureau of Labor Statistics.*

Tyson, W. (2011). Modeling engineering degree attainment using high school and college

    physics and calculus coursetaking and achievement. *Journal of Engineering*

    *Education, 100*(4), 760–777. https://doi-org.nl.idm.oclc.org/10.1002/j.2168-

    9830.2011.tb00035.x

Tyson, W., Lee, R., Borman, K. M., & Hanson, M. A. (2007). Science, technology, engineering,

    and mathematics (STEM) pathways: High school science and math coursework and

    postsecondary degree attainment. *Journal of Education for Students Placed at*

    *Risk, 12*(3), 243–270. https://doi-org.nl.idm.oclc.org/10.1080/10824660701601266

U.S. Census (2017). Facts for Features: Hispanic Heritage Month 2017. U.S. Census. Retrieved

    from https://www.census.gov/newsroom/facts-for-features/2017/hispanic-heritage.html

U.S. Census (2010). 2010 Census Shows Asians are Fastest-Growing Race Group. U.S. Census

    Retrieved from https://www.census.gov/newsroom/releases/archives/2010_census/cb12-

    cn22.html

Xue, Y. & Larson, R. C. (2015). STEM crisis or STEM surplus? yes and yes. *Monthly Labor*

    *Review,* 14-1B,2B,3B,4B,5B,6B,7B,8B,9B,10B,11B,12B,13B,14B

Wax, A. L. (2017). Educating the disadvantaged-two models. *Harvard Journal of Law and*

    *Public Policy, 40*(3), 687-728.

Webb, N. (1997). Criteria for alignment of expectations and assessments in mathematics and science education. *National Institute for Science Education*. Retrieved from https://files.eric.ed.gov/fulltext/ED414305.pdf

Wisdom, S., Leavitt, L. (2015). *Handbook of Research on Advancing Critical Thinking in Higher Education*, Hershey: Information Science Reference.

World Economic Forum (2018). In countries with higher gender equality, women are less likely to get STEM degrees. Retrieved from https://www.weforum.org/agenda/2018/02/does-gender-equality-result-in-fewer-female-stem-grads

The World Bank (2019). Improving the pathway from school to STEM careers for girls and women. Retrieved from https://blogs.worldbank.org/opendata/improving-pathway-school-stem-careers-girls-and-women

Wang, X. (2013). Why students choose STEM majors: Motivation, high school learning, and postsecondary context of support. *American Educational Research Journal* 50(5):1081–1121.

Wang, Y., Rodriguez de Gil, P., Chen, Y., Kromrey, J., Kim, E., Pham, T., Nguyen, D., & Romano, J. (2017). Comparing the performance of approaches for testing the homogeneity of variance assumption in one-factor ANOVA models. *Educational and Psychological Measurements*, 77(2), pg. 305-329

Zhu, J. & Cox, M. F. (2015). Epistemological development profiles of Chinese engineering doctoral students in U.S. institutions: An application of Perry's theory. *Journal of Engineering Education*, [s. l.], v. 104, n. 3, p. 345–362, 2015.

Appendix A

Figure 1

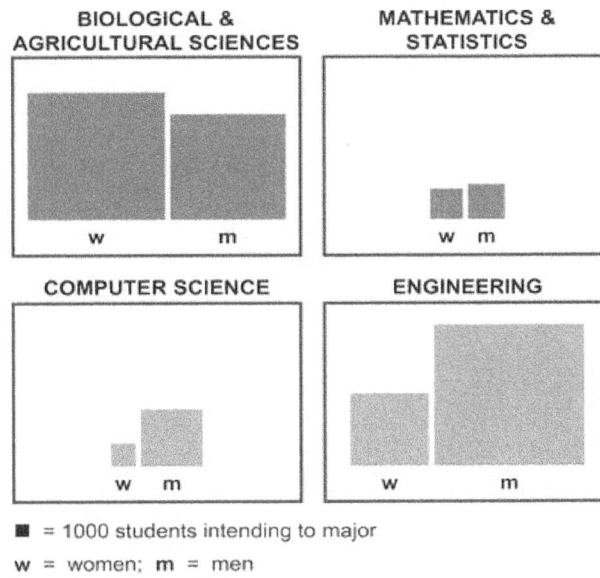

= 1000 students intending to major

w = women; m = men

*Number of female and male freshmen intending to major in STEM fields in 2010. SOURCE: National Science Foundation (2012). Raw numbers based on weightings from Pryor et al. (2010).*

Appendix B

Figure 2

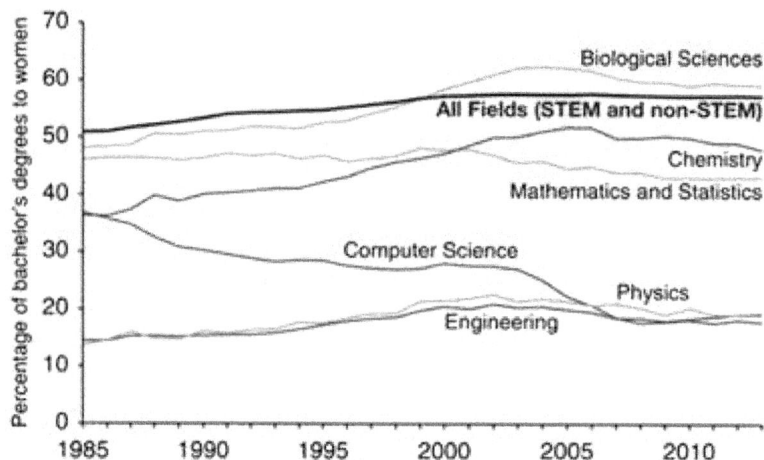

Percentage of bachelor's degrees awarded to women in STEM fields from 1985-2013. SOURCE: National Science Foundation, National Center for Science and Engineering Statistics, Integrated Science and Engineering Resources Data System (WebCASPAR). https://webcaspar.nsf.gov

Appendix C

Figure 3

## Despite higher enrollment in tertiary, women are less likely to major in STEM fields

Student enrollment by career program (%)

■ Male  ■ Female

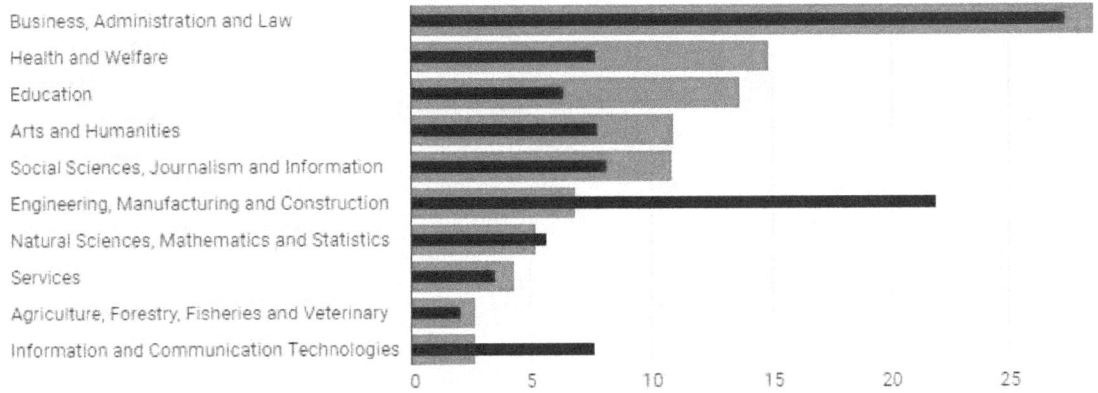

Source: UNESCO Institute for Statistics

Appendix D

Figure 4

Average scores of 15-year-old students on the PISA mathematics literacy scale, by education system: 2015

| Education system | Average score | | s.e. | Education system | Average score | | s.e. |
|---|---|---|---|---|---|---|---|
| OECD average | 490 | ⚪ | 0.4 | Israel | 470 | | 3.6 |
| Singapore | 564 | ⚪ | 1.5 | United States | 470 | | 3.2 |
| Hong Kong (China) | 548 | ⚪ | 3.0 | Croatia | 464 | | 2.8 |
| Macau (China) | 544 | ⚪ | 1.1 | Buenos Aires (Argentina) | 456 | | 6.9 |
| Chinese Taipei | 542 | ⚪ | 3.0 | Greece | 454 | ▼ | 3.8 |
| Japan | 532 | ⚪ | 3.0 | Romania | 444 | ▼ | 3.8 |
| B-S-J-G (China) | 531 | ⚪ | 4.9 | Bulgaria | 441 | ▼ | 4.0 |
| Korea, Republic of | 524 | ⚪ | 3.7 | Cyprus | 437 | ▼ | 1.7 |
| Switzerland | 521 | ⚪ | 2.9 | United Arab Emirates | 427 | ▼ | 2.4 |
| Estonia | 520 | ⚪ | 2.0 | Chile | 423 | ▼ | 2.5 |
| Canada | 516 | ⚪ | 2.3 | Turkey | 420 | ▼ | 4.1 |
| Netherlands | 512 | ⚪ | 2.2 | Moldova, Republic of | 420 | ▼ | 2.5 |
| Denmark | 511 | ⚪ | 2.2 | Uruguay | 418 | ▼ | 2.5 |
| Finland | 511 | ⚪ | 2.3 | Montenegro, Republic of | 418 | ▼ | 1.5 |
| Slovenia | 510 | ⚪ | 1.3 | Trinidad and Tobago | 417 | ▼ | 1.4 |
| Belgium | 507 | ⚪ | 2.4 | Thailand | 415 | ▼ | 3.0 |
| Germany | 506 | ⚪ | 2.9 | Albania | 413 | ▼ | 3.4 |
| Poland | 504 | ⚪ | 2.4 | Mexico | 408 | ▼ | 2.2 |
| Ireland | 504 | ⚪ | 2.1 | Georgia | 404 | ▼ | 2.8 |
| Norway | 502 | ⚪ | 2.2 | Qatar | 402 | ▼ | 1.3 |
| Austria | 497 | ⚪ | 2.9 | Costa Rica | 400 | ▼ | 2.5 |
| New Zealand | 495 | ⚪ | 2.3 | Lebanon | 396 | ▼ | 3.7 |
| Vietnam | 495 | ⚪ | 4.5 | Colombia | 390 | ▼ | 2.3 |
| Russian Federation | 494 | ⚪ | 3.1 | Peru | 387 | ▼ | 2.7 |
| Sweden | 494 | ⚪ | 3.2 | Indonesia | 386 | ▼ | 3.1 |
| Australia | 494 | ⚪ | 1.6 | Jordan | 380 | ▼ | 2.7 |
| France | 493 | ⚪ | 2.1 | Brazil | 377 | ▼ | 2.9 |
| United Kingdom | 492 | ⚪ | 2.5 | Macedonia, Republic of | 371 | ▼ | 1.3 |
| Czech Republic | 492 | ⚪ | 2.4 | Tunisia | 367 | ▼ | 3.0 |
| Portugal | 492 | ⚪ | 2.5 | Kosovo | 362 | ▼ | 1.6 |
| Italy | 490 | ⚪ | 2.8 | Algeria | 360 | ▼ | 3.0 |
| Iceland | 488 | ⚪ | 2.0 | Dominican Republic | 328 | ▼ | 2.7 |
| Spain | 486 | ⚪ | 2.2 | | | | |
| Luxembourg | 486 | ⚪ | 1.3 | | | | |
| Latvia | 482 | ⚪ | 1.9 | | | | |
| Malta | 479 | ⚪ | 1.7 | U.S. states and territories | | | |
| Lithuania | 478 | ⚪ | 2.3 | Massachusetts | 500 | ⚪ | 5.5 |
| Hungary | 477 | | 2.5 | North Carolina | 471 | | 4.4 |
| Slovak Republic | 475 | | 2.7 | Puerto Rico | 378 | ▼ | 5.6 |

⚪ Average score is higher than U.S. average score at the .05 level of statistical significance.
▼ Average score is lower than U.S. average score at the .05 level of statistical significance.

Source: PISA International 2015

Appendix E

Figure 5

The distribution of international tertiary new entrants by field of education in 2010
for Australia, and a selection of comparable countries

| Country | Engineering, manufacturing and construction | Sciences | Mathematics and statistics | Computing | Other |
|---|---|---|---|---|---|
| Sweden | 34.51% | 8.60% | 1.90% | 6.73% | 48.26% |
| Finland | 31.72% | 3.67% | 0.46% | 7.03% | 57.13% |
| Germany | 21.58% | 7.05% | 1.93% | 7.30% | 62.14% |
| United States | 18.42% | 8.77% | 2.08% | 6.64% | 64.09% |
| Canada | 15.75% | 7.75% | 2.74% | 4.94% | 68.82% |
| Denmark | 19.27% | 1.71% | 2.06% | 6.54% | 70.42% |
| United Kingdom | 14.88% | 5.73% | 1.78% | 6.14% | 71.46% |
| New Zealand | 6.99% | 6.91% | 2.45% | 9.79% | 73.87% |
| Australia | 11.08% | 3.48% | 0.47% | 7.65% | 77.33% |
| Japan | 14.98% | 1.21% | 0.00% | 0.00% | 83.81% |

Source: OECD 2012a, *Education at a Glance 2012: OECD Indicators*, OECD Publishing, Paris.

Appendix F

Figure 6

**Over 17 million workers are employed in STEM occupations**

*Employed adults ages 25 and older, in millions*

| | |
|---|---|
| All employed | 131.3 |
| STEM employed | 17.3 |
| Healthcare practitioners/technicians | 9.0 |
| Computer workers | 4.4 |
| Engineers/architects | 2.7 |
| Physical scientists | 0.6 |
| Life scientists | 0.3 |
| Mathematical workers | 0.2 |
| Non-STEM employed | 114.0 |

Note: Figures do not add to totals indicated due to rounding. STEM stands for science, technology, engineering and math.
Source: Pew Research Center analysis of 2014-2016 American Community Survey (IPUMS).
"Women and Men in STEM Often at Odds Over Workplace Equity"

**PEW RESEARCH CENTER**

Appendix G

Figure 7

## The Asian population in the U.S. has grown 72% since 2000

*In thousands*

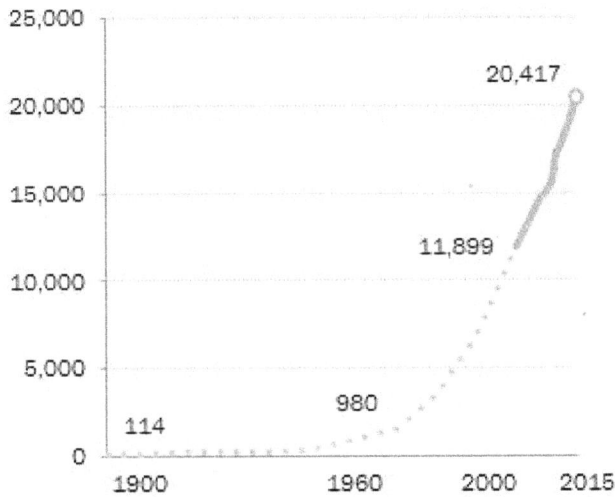

Note: In 2000 and later, Asians include the mixed-race and mixed-group populations, regardless of Hispanic origin. Prior to 2000, the census only allowed one race category to be selected. Asians include Pacific Islanders in 1980 and earlier years.

Source: 2000 and 2010 population estimates from U.S. Census Bureau, "The Asian Population: 2010" Census Brief, Table 6. For 2006-2009 and 2011-2015, American Community Survey 1-year estimates (American Fact Finder). For 1990, U.S. Census Bureau, "Asian Population: 2000" Census Brief, Table 2. For 1980 and earlier years, Campbell Gibson and Kay Jung, "Historical Census Statistics on Population Totals by Race, 1790 to 1990, and by Hispanic Origin, 1970 to 1990, for the United States, Regions, Divisions and States," U.S. Census Bureau

PEW RESEARCH CENTER

Appendix H

Figure 8  STEM Entrants for Bachelor Degree

| Percentage of 2003–04 beginning bachelor's and associate's degree students who entered but subsequently left STEM fields, by demographic, precollege academic, and postsecondary enrollment characteristics: 2003–2009 | | | | |
|---|---|---|---|---|
| | STEM entrants among beginning bachelor's degree students | | STEM entrants among beginning associate's degree students | |
| Demographic, precollege academic, and postsecondary enrollment characteristics | Left PSE without a degree or certificate[a] | Switched major to a non-STEM field | Left PSE without a degree or certificate[a] | Switched major to a non-STEM field |
| Total | 20.2 | 28.1 | 36.5 | 32.6 |
| Sex | | | | |
| Male | 23.7 | 25.5 | 38.0 | 28.8 |
| Female | 14.2 | 32.4 | 32.7 | 42.6 |
| Race/ethnicity[2] | | | | |
| White | 19.6 | 28.1 | 35.6 | 30.3 |
| Black | 29.3 | 36.0 | 41.5 | 36.3 |
| Hispanic | 23.1 | 26.4 | 39.9 | 37.6 |
| Asian | 9.6 | 22.6 | 26.2 | 28.1 |
| All other races | 20.5 | 25.4 | 33.4 ! | 46.9 |
| Highest education of parents | | | | |
| High school or less | 30.1 | 28.8 | 35.6 | 34.2 |
| Some college | 22.1 | 27.2 | 42.1 | 31.6 |
| Bachelor's degree or higher | 16.6 | 27.9 | 31.6 | 32.6 |
| Income level in 2003–04[3] | | | | |
| Lowest 25 percent | 29.2 | 28.6 | 45.9 | 25.1 |
| Lower middle 25 percent | 21.6 | 28.4 | 27.6 | 38.8 |
| Upper middle 25 percent | 18.2 | 27.6 | 29.6 | 34.1 |
| Highest 25 percent | 15.4 | 28.0 | 42.6 | 34.1 |
| Highest mathematics in high school[4] | | | | |
| Skipped | 46.9 | 27.1 ! | 46.6 | 28.1 |
| None of the following | 40.6 | 17.4 ! | 47.1 | 24.3 |
| Algebra II/trigonometry | 28.7 | 32.6 | 31.0 | 38.9 |
| Pre-calculus | 19.6 | 32.1 | 27.3 | 32.6 |
| Calculus | 12.6 | 23.7 | 28.7 | 37.1 ! |
| High school GPA[4] | | | | |
| Skipped | 33.2 | 26.9 | 40.6 | 30.8 |
| Less than 2.50 | 45.6 | 25.3 ! | 41.6 | 36.3 |
| 2.50–2.99 | 24.6 | 32.9 | 37.6 | 30.4 |
| 3.00–3.49 | 22.1 | 32.6 | 36.2 | 31.3 |
| 3.50 or higher | 14.4 | 28.6 | 21.8 | 36.8 |

Appendix I

Figure 9  Rates of return on parental expenditures on children

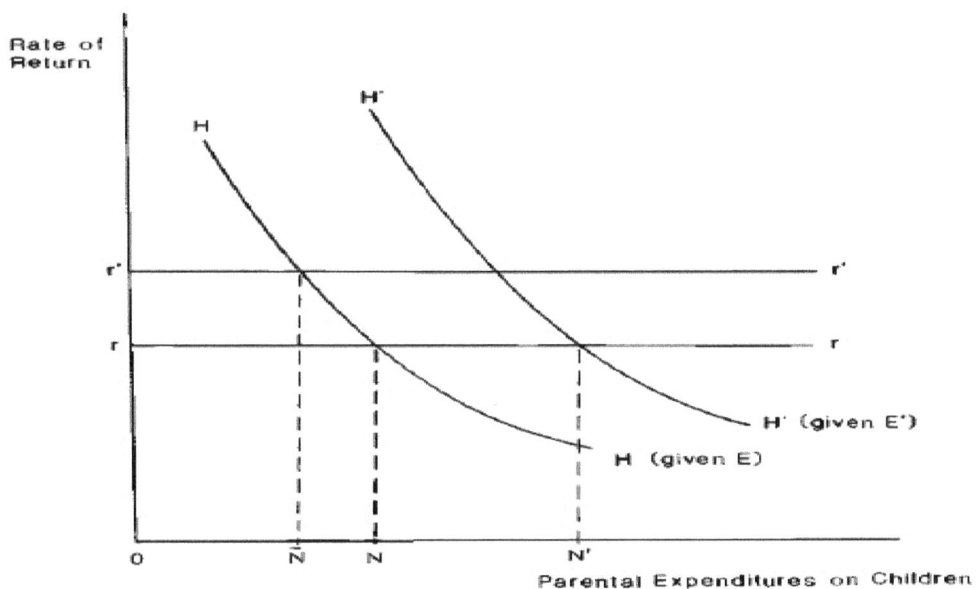

Note.  The horizontal supply curve (r, r') intersects with a negatively declined demand curve (H, H'). More financial endowed children tend to accumulate more human capital. The endowed are represented by E, and E' > E. The notation of N and N' represents public expenditures. Source: (Becker, & Tomes, 1985).

Appendix J

Figure 10

Income Shares, Income Inequality, and Income Mobility

2010 census race and ethnicity data matched to Form 1040, ages 25–65

| | 2010 Census Count (1) | % (2) | 2010 Census PIK Number (3) | % (4) | 2010 Census–IRS Match Amount (5) | IRS Match 2010 Census % (6) | Final Data Set (7) |
|---|---|---|---|---|---|---|---|
| Number of Observations | 166,305,994 | 100.0 | 151,565,180 | 91.1 | 123,783,849 | 74.4 | 100.0 |
| Sex | | | | | | | |
| Male | 82,083,737 | 49.4 | 74,069,567 | 90.2 | 58,876,049 | 71.7 | 47.6 |
| Female | 84,222,257 | 50.6 | 77,495,613 | 92.0 | 64,907,800 | 77.1 | 52.4 |
| Age Group | | | | | | | |
| 25-44 | 82,123,330 | 49.4 | 73,362,250 | 89.3 | 60,402,428 | 73.6 | 48.8 |
| 45-64 | 84,182,664 | 50.6 | 78,202,930 | 92.9 | 63,381,421 | 75.3 | 51.2 |
| Race | | | | | | | |
| White | 109,396,016 | 65.8 | 102,361,646 | 93.6 | 86,622,296 | 79.2 | 70.0 |
| Hispanic | 24,631,312 | 14.8 | 20,572,899 | 83.5 | 15,852,995 | 64.4 | 12.8 |
| Black | 19,832,168 | 11.9 | 17,468,337 | 88.1 | 12,080,486 | 60.9 | 9.8 |
| AIAN[a] | 1,174,014 | 0.7 | 1,024,411 | 87.3 | 698,199 | 59.5 | 0.6 |
| Asian | 8,530,347 | 5.1 | 7,686,570 | 90.1 | 6,667,599 | 78.2 | 5.4 |
| NHPI[b] | 255,324 | 0.2 | 216,815 | 84.9 | 165,558 | 64.8 | 0.1 |
| Other | 2,486,813 | 1.5 | 2,234,502 | 89.9 | 1,696,716 | 68.2 | 1.4 |

Source: (Akee, Jones, & Porter, 2019).

Appendix K

Figure 11

Shares of income by race, 2000 and 2014

| | Overall Total (%) | As a Percentage of Row Total | | | | | | |
| | | White | Hispanic | Black | AIAN[a] | Asian | NHPI[b] | Other |
|---|---|---|---|---|---|---|---|---|
| A. 2000 | | | | | | | | |
| Top | | | | | | | | |
| 10 % | 40.79 | 89.73 | 2.46 | 2.11 | 0.25 | 5.26 | 0.07 | 0.13 |
| 1 % | 17.87 | 92.10 | 1.88 | 0.97 | 0.19 | 4.67 | 0.06 | 0.13 |
| 0.1 % | 8.85 | 92.53 | 1.65 | 0.95 | 0.16 | 4.54 | 0.06 | 0.12 |
| Bottom | | | | | | | | |
| 10 % | 1.20 | 54.88 | 19.57 | 18.18 | 1.56 | 5.32 | 0.23 | 0.27 |
| 1 % | 0.02 | 59.51 | 13.13 | 19.66 | 2.00 | 5.18 | 0.25 | 0.26 |
| Population percentage | | 75.13 | 9.61 | 9.72 | 0.84 | 4.37 | 0.17 | 0.18 |
| B. 2014 | | | | | | | | |
| Top | | | | | | | | |
| 10 % | 40.31 | 84.13 | 4.10 | 2.76 | 0.33 | 8.40 | 0.08 | 0.20 |
| 1 % | 16.01 | 87.83 | 3.13 | 1.39 | 0.25 | 7.16 | 0.05 | 0.19 |
| 0.1 % | 7.35 | 89.10 | 2.75 | 1.37 | 0.21 | 6.35 | 0.04 | 0.18 |
| Bottom | | | | | | | | |
| 10 % | 1.00 | 50.68 | 20.35 | 21.42 | 1.39 | 5.53 | 0.30 | 0.32 |
| 1 % | 0.01 | 66.18 | 12.03 | 14.34 | 1.57 | 5.32 | 0.25 | 0.30 |
| Population percentage | | 69.48 | 12.79 | 10.67 | 0.85 | 5.74 | 0.22 | 0.23 |

*Notes:* The table reports the total income share accruing to persons within the percentage of the income distribution reported in the row, broken out by race and ethnicity. Population percentages are reported for comparison.

*Source:* Race and ethnicity file—Form 1040 data, 2000 and 2014.

[a] AIAN = American Indian or Alaska Native.

[b] NHPI = Native Hawaiian or Other Pacific Islander.

Source: (Akee, Jones, & Porter, 2019).

Appendix L

Figure 12                    Implicit Theoretical Model

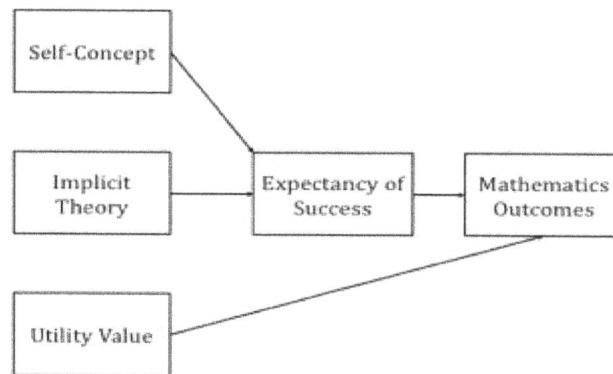

Note. Implicit theoretical model links self-concept and expectancy to math outcomes.

Appendix M

Figure 13

Largest Opportunity Occupations (2017)

| | | | Distribution of Total Occupational Employment | | |
|---|---|---|---|---|---|
| Occupation Title | Opportunity Employment | Share of Sub-Baccalaureate Job Ads | Opportunity Employment | Higher Wages, Bachelor's Degree Required | Lower Wages |
| Registered Nurses | 1,374,014 | 65.9% | 65.9% | 34.1% | 0.0% |
| Heavy and Tractor-Trailer Truck Drivers | 1,032,790 | 100.0% | 93.1% | 0.0% | 6.9% |
| Bookkeeping, Accounting, and Auditing Clerks | 581,455 | 58.8% | 52.8% | 37.4% | 9.8% |
| Maintenance and Repair Workers | 491,285 | 100.0% | 54.0% | 0.0% | 46.0% |
| Carpenters | 457,460 | 100.0% | 91.7% | 0.0% | 8.3% |
| Electricians | 453,790 | 100.0% | 100.0% | 0.0% | 0.0% |
| Licensed Practical and Licensed Vocational Nurses | 446,360 | 100.0% | 100.0% | 0.0% | 0.0% |
| Supervisors of Office and Administrative Support Workers | 433,025 | 38.9% | 39.5% | 60.5% | 0.0% |
| General and Operations Managers | 432,315 | 24.6% | 26.0% | 74.0% | 0.0% |
| Sales Representatives, Wholesale and Manufacturing | 426,495 | 39.5% | 40.3% | 59.5% | 0.3% |
| Police and Sheriff's Patrol Officers | 405,652 | 89.0% | 87.9% | 12.1% | 0.0% |
| Sales Representatives, Services, All Other | 370,776 | 44.9% | 45.0% | 53.8% | 1.2% |
| Supervisors of Retail Sales Workers | 368,040 | 64.9% | 45.1% | 21.3% | 33.7% |
| Automotive Service Technicians and Mechanics | 338,550 | 100.0% | 76.9% | 0.0% | 23.1% |
| Plumbers, Pipefitters, and Steamfitters | 313,670 | 100.0% | 99.7% | 0.0% | 0.3% |
| Secretaries and Administrative Assistants | 284,418 | 73.6% | 17.7% | 5.1% | 77.2% |
| Construction Laborers | 270,250 | 100.0% | 40.2% | 0.0% | 59.8% |
| Computer User Support Specialists | 262,827 | 53.1% | 52.6% | 47.1% | 0.3% |
| Supervisors of Construction Trades and Extraction Workers | 254,647 | 65.9% | 65.3% | 34.7% | 0.0% |
| Executive Secretaries and Executive Administrative Assistants | 227,786 | 46.0% | 47.3% | 52.7% | 0.0% |
| Securities, Commodities, and Financial Services Sales Agents | 225,101 | 70.8% | 66.9% | 32.1% | 1.0% |
| Heating, Air Conditioning, and Refrigeration Mechanics and Installers | 221,640 | 100.0% | 100.0% | 0.0% | 0.0% |
| Supervisors of Mechanics, Installers, and Repairers | 204,586 | 65.4% | 65.5% | 34.5% | 0.0% |
| Supervisors of Transportation and Material Moving Workers | 204,286 | 71.8% | 72.0% | 28.0% | 0.0% |
| Supervisors of Production and Operating Workers | 202,699 | 53.5% | 53.5% | 46.5% | 0.0% |

Sources: Authors' calculations using data from BLS Occupational Employment Statistics (May 2017), Burning Glass Technologies (2015–2017), BEA Regional Price Parities (2016), and American Community Survey Five-Year Public Use Microdata Sample (2012–2016)

Appendix N

Figure 14  Math Completion of Whites & African-America

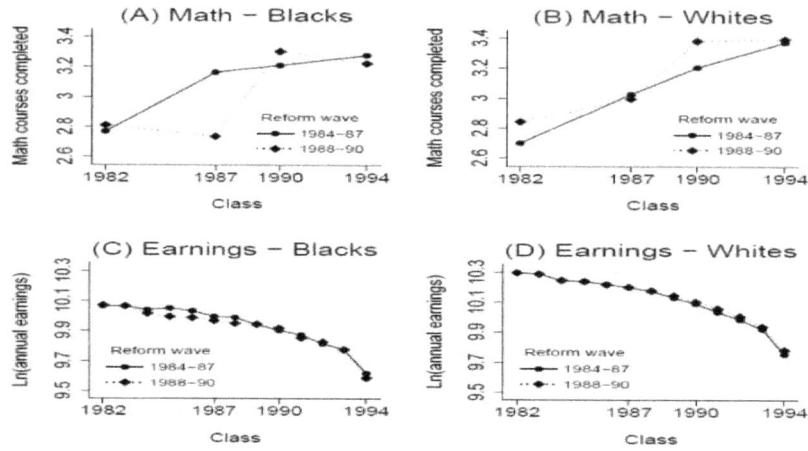

Note.  Whites take more rigorous math classes than African-Americans (Blacks) and earn more money.

Appendix O

Figure 15

**Black men have low earnings mobility**

Share of youths from the bottom quintile who remain in the bottom quintile as adults

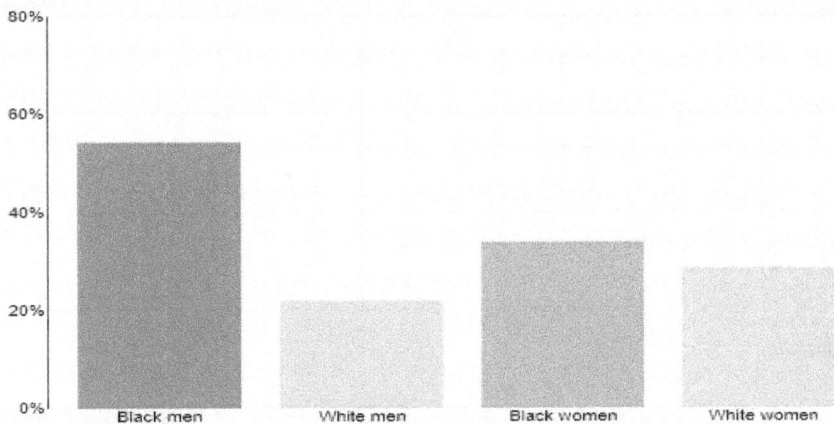

Source: Authors' calculations using the NLSY97                    BROOKINGS

Appendix P

Consent to Participate in Research

NATIONAL
LOUIS
UNIVERSITY
1886    ACCESS. INNOVATION. EXCELLENCE.

Office of the Provost
122 South Michigan Avenue
Chicago, Illinois 60603-6162

www.nl.edu
P/F 312.261.3729

Kendall E. Coleman

Dear Kendall E. Coleman:

The Institutional Review Board (IRB) has received your application for your research study "Minority Students in STEM Careers in the U.S.: The Role of AP Calculus" IRB has noted that your application is complete and that your study has been approved by your primary advisor and an IRB representative. Your application has been filed as Exempt in the Office of the Provost.

Please note that the approval for your study is for one year, from August 3, 2019 to August 3, 2020. As you carry out your research, you must report any adverse events or reactions to the IRB.

At the end of your approved year, please inform the IRB in writing of the status of the study (i.e. complete, continuing). During this time, if your study changes in ways that impact human participants differently or more significantly than indicated in the current application, please submit a Change of Research Study form to the IRB, which may be found on NLU's IRB website.

All good wishes for the successful completion of your research.

Sincerely,

Shaunti Knauth, Ph.D.
Chair, IRB

## Appendix Q

## Codebook Parent's Education

```
File:      STUDENT
Name:      X2PAREDU
Position:  869
Length:    2
Label:     X2 Parents'/guardians' highest level of education
```

Description:
Indicates the highest level of education achieved by either parent 1 or parent 2. X2PAREDU is constructed from two composite variables (X2PAR1EDU and X2PAR2EDU) which can contain imputed values; if either of these two input variables are imputed and the highest level of education could not be inferred from non-imputed data, then the imputation flag for X2PAREDU (X2PAREDU_IM) is set to 2. Unit nonresponse for this composite is less than the set of F1 student nonrespondents (X2SQSTAT>7) due to inclusion of parent data for student nonrespondents and questionnaire incapables. The additional parent data are available for use with the W2PARENT weight.

SAS Logic:
```
if X2PQSTAT in (8,9) then X2PAREDU = -8 ;
else if X2PAR1EDU=7 or X2PAR2EDU=7 then X2PAREDU=7;
else if X2PAR1EDU=-9 or X2PAR2EDU=-9 then X2PAREDU=-9;
else if X2PAR1EDU >= X2PAR2EDU then X2PAREDU = X2PAR1EDU ;
else if X2PAR2EDU > 0 then X2PAREDU = X2PAR2EDU ;
```

| Category | Label | Frequency Unweighted | Percent Unweighted |
|---|---|---|---|
| 1 | Less than high school | 1,094 | 4.65 |
| 2 | High school diploma or GED or alterntive HS credential | 6,400 | 27.23 |
| 3 | Certificate/diploma from school providing occupational training | 1,011 | 4.30 |
| 4 | Associate's degree | 3,342 | 14.22 |
| 5 | Bachelor's degree | 5,154 | 21.93 |
| 6 | Master's degree | 2,615 | 11.13 |
| 7 | Ph.D/M.D/Law/other high lvl prof degree | 1,303 | 5.54 |
| -8 | Unit non-response | 2,584 | 10.99 |
| TOTAL | | 23,503 | 100.00 |

## Appendix R

## Codebook Mom's Education

File:      STUDENT

Name:      X2MOMEDU

Position:  877

Length:    2

Label:     X2 Mother's/female guardian's highest level of education


Description:

For sample members who have a biological, adoptive, or step mother living in their household, X2MOMEDU indicates the highest level of education achieved by that biological, adoptive, or step mother identified in the first-followup parent questionnaire. X2MOMEDU is derived from four composite variables (X2P1RELATION, X2P2RELATION, X2PAR1EDU, and X2PAR2EDU) which can contain imputed values; if any of these four input variables are imputed, then the imputation flag for X2MOMEDU (X2MOMEDU_IM) is set to 2.


SAS Logic:
if X2PQSTAT in (8,9) then X2MOMEDU = -8 ;
else if X2P1RELATION = 1 then X2MOMEDU = X2PAR1EDU ;
else if X2P2RELATION = 1 then X2MOMEDU = X2PAR2EDU ;
else if X2P1RELATION = 3 then X2MOMEDU = X2PAR1EDU ;
else if X2P2RELATION = 3 then X2MOMEDU = X2PAR2EDU ;
else if X2P1RELATION = 5 then X2MOMEDU = X2PAR1EDU ;
else if X2P2RELATION = 5 then X2MOMEDU = X2PAR2EDU ;
else if X2P1RELATION in (2 4 6 7 8 9 10 11 12 13 14 15 16) and
     X2P2RELATION in (2 4 6 7 8 9 10 11 12 13 14 15 16 -7) then X2MOMEDU = 0 ;
else if X2MOMREL = -9 then X2MOMEDU = -9;
else X2MOMEDU = -9 ;


| Category | Label | Frequency Unweighted | Percent Unweighted |
|----------|-------|----------------------|--------------------|
| 0 | No bio/adoptive/step-mother in household | 1,530 | 6.51 |
| 1 | Less than high school | 1,576 | 6.71 |
| 2 | High school diploma or GED or alternative HS credential | 7,160 | 30.46 |
| 3 | Certificate/diploma from school providing occupational training | 829 | 3.53 |
| 4 | Associate's degree | 3,108 | 13.22 |
| 5 | Bachelor's degree | 4,476 | 19.04 |
| 6 | Master's degree | 1,674 | 7.12 |
| 7 | Ph.D./M.D/Law/other high lvl prof degree | 566 | 2.41 |
| -8 | Unit non-response | 2,584 | 10.99 |
| TOTAL | | 23,503 | 100.00 |

Appendix S

Codebook Dad's Education

File:           STUDENT
Name:           X2DADEDU
Position:       895
Length:         2
Label:          X2 Father's/male guardian's highest level of education

Description:
For sample members who have a biological, adoptive, or step father living in their household,
X2DADEDU indicates the highest level of education achieved by that biological, adoptive, or step
father identified in the first follow-up parent questionnaire. X2DADEDU is derived from four
composite variables (X2P1RELATION, X2P2RELATION, X2PAR1EDU, and X2PAR2EDU) which contain
imputed values; if any of these four input variables are imputed, then the imputation flag for
X2DADEDU (X2DADEDU_IM) is set to 2.

SAS Logic:
if X2PQSTAT in (8,9) then X2DADEDU = -8 ;
else if X2P1RELATION = 2 then X2DADEDU = X2PAR1EDU ;
else if X2P2RELATION = 2 then X2DADEDU = X2PAR2EDU ;
else if X2P1RELATION = 4 then X2DADEDU = X2PAR1EDU ;
else if X2P2RELATION = 4 then X2DADEDU = X2PAR2EDU ;
else if X2P1RELATION = 6 then X2DADEDU = X2PAR1EDU ;
else if X2P2RELATION = 6 then X2DADEDU = X2PAR2EDU ;
else if X2P1RELATION in (  1 3 5 7 8 9 10 11 12 13 14 15 16) and
    X2P2RELATION in (-7  1 3 5 7 8 9 10 11 12 13 14 15 16) then X2DADEDU = 0 ;
else if X2DADREL = -9 then X2DADEDU = -9;
else X2DADEDU = -9 ;

| Category | Label | Frequency Unweighted | Percent Unweighted |
|---|---|---|---|
| 0 | No bio/adoptive/step-father in household | 5,193 | 22.10 |
| 1 | Less than high school | 1,461 | 6.22 |
| 2 | High school diploma or GED or alternative HS credential | 6,151 | 26.17 |
| 3 | Certificate/diploma from school providing occupational training | 557 | 2.37 |
| 4 | Associate's degree | 1,941 | 8.26 |
| 5 | Bachelor's degree | 3,333 | 14.18 |
| 6 | Master's degree | 1,411 | 6.00 |
| 7 | Ph.D/M.D/Law/other high lvl prof degree | 872 | 3.71 |
| -8 | Unit non-response | 2,584 | 10.99 |
| TOTAL | | 23,503 | 100.00 |

Appendix T

Codebook At Least One Credit Earned in Calculus

File:       STUDENT
Name:       X3T1CREDCALC
Position:   1266
Length:     2
Label:      X3 At least one credit earned in: calculus

Description:
Indicates at least one Carnegie unit in Calculus, which is the course SCED code(s): 02121, 02122, 02123, 02126.
A Carnegie unit is equivalent to a one-year academic course taken one period a day, five days a week.

SAS Logic:
if T3SSCED in ('02121','02122','02123','02126') and T3SGRLEV >= 4 then X3T1CREDCALC = X3T1CREDCALC + T3SCRED;
if X3T1CREDCALC >= .99 then X3T1CREDCALC = 1;
else X3T1CREDCALC = 0;

| Category | Label | Frequency Unweighted | Percent Unweighted |
|---|---|---|---|
| 0 | No | 18,468 | 78.58 |
| 1 | Yes | 3,460 | 14.72 |
| -8 | Unit non-response | 1,575 | 6.70 |
| TOTAL | | 23,503 | 100.00 |

## *Notes*

# *Notes*

# *Notes*

## *Notes*

## *Notes*

_**Notes**_

***Notes***

## *Notes*

*Notes*

# *Notes*

*Notes*

## <u>*Notes*</u>

### *Notes*

## *Notes*

## *Notes*

*<u>Notes</u>*

**You may write letters to Dr. Coleman at**

Dr. Kendall E. Coleman

P.O. Box 19381

7715 S. Cottage Grove Ave. Suite 1

Chicago, IL 60619

www.ingramcontent.com/pod-product-compliance
Lightning Source LLC
Chambersburg PA
CBHW081215020426

42331CB00012B/3035